Applied International
Finance II

Applied International Finance II

International Cost of Capital and Capital Budgeting

Second Edition

Thomas J. O'Brien

BUSINESS EXPERT PRESS

Applied International Finance II: International Cost of Capital and Capital Budgeting, Second Edition

First published in 2014 by
Business Expert Press, LLC
222 East 46th Street, New York, NY 10017
www.businessexpertpress.com

ISBN-13: 978-1-63157-922-6 (paperback)
ISBN-13: 978-1-63157-923-3 (e-book)

Business Expert Press Finance and Financial Management Collection

Collection ISSN: 2331-0049 (print)
Collection ISSN: 2331-0057 (electronic)

Cover and interior design by Exeter Premedia Services Private Ltd., Chennai, India

Second edition: 2017

10 9 8 7 6 5 4 3 2 1

Printed in the United States of America.

Abstract

This volume is part of a three-volume set designed for use in applied international corporate finance courses for students, managers, and executives. Instead of an "encyclopedic" approach, the volumes focus on the main interests of managers who deal with international finance issues. This volume's issue is the cost of capital in international financial markets, hurdle rates for overseas operations, cross-border valuation, and international capital budgeting applications. The volume contains a hypothetical case that aims to tie the material together. The case company is evaluating an overseas expansion proposal and whether to locate the manufacturing facility in the home country or the overseas country. This volume reviews some basics of foreign exchange rates; for more information, see the first volume: Thomas J. O'Brien, *Introduction to Foreign Exchange Rates*, 2nd edition, Business Expert Press, 2016. The second volume deals how uncertain foreign exchange rate changes affect a firm's ongoing cash flows and equity value, and what can be done about this risk: Thomas J. O'Brien, *Applied International Finance I: Managing Foreign Exchange Risk*, 2nd edition, Business Expert Press, 2017.

Keywords

beta, capital budgeting, CAPM, cost of capital, cross-border valuation, currency index, foreign exchange (FX) exposure, global CAPM, hurdle rates, international CAPM, risk premium

Contents

Acknowledgments

I thank Shmuel Baruch, Reid Click, Demissew Ejara, Martin Glaum, John Griffin, Alain Krapl, Steve Magee, Chris Malone, Dev Mishra, and Santiago Ruiz de Vargas for their helpful comments and discussions. I also thank UConn students in my International Finance classes over the years for helpful editing and feedback.

Review of Foreign Exchange Rates

A foreign exchange (FX) rate is, simply, the price of one currency in terms of another. An FX rate between US dollars and British pounds can be expressed as either (a) US dollars per British pound or (b) British pounds per US dollar. We use the notation 2 \$/£ to mean 2 US dollars (\$2) per British pound, or that \$2 will buy 1 British pound. Equivalently, we can use the reciprocal, 0.50 £/\$, which means 0.50 British pounds (£0.50) per US dollar, or that £0.50 will buy 1 US dollar.

An FX rate expresses the price of the "denominator currency" in terms of the "numerator currency." The numerator currency is called the *pricing currency*, or the *terms currency*. The denominator currency is sometimes called the *base currency*. **Always remember that when we use the expression "FX price of such-and-such currency," we are thinking in terms of that currency as the "denominator currency,"** and we are expressing its price in terms of the "numerator currency." Thus, 2 \$/£ expresses the FX price of the British pound versus the US dollar (the pricing currency), and 0.50 £/\$ expresses the FX price of the US dollar versus the British pound (the pricing currency).

In financial markets, FX rate quotes often involve the US dollar as one of the two currencies. The usual convention is to quote the FX rate with the US dollar as the base currency. The common FX market convention to quote the FX price of the US dollar is called *European terms*, although the pricing currency involved is not necessarily a European currency. The convention to quote most FX rates in European terms emerged after World War II, when the US dollar replaced the British pound as the principal international currency. The FX rates expressed the price of 1 US dollar in terms of the currency of each country, many of which were European. For example, an FX quote of 1.20 in the case of the Swiss franc (the "Swissie") implies 1.20 Swiss francs per US dollar, or 1.20 Sf/\$, and an FX quote of 108 for the Japanese yen means 108 yen per US dollar, or 108 ¥/\$.

Although most FX rates are conventionally quoted in European terms, a few important currencies are typically quoted with the US dollar as the pricing currency. This style is referred to as *American terms*. An FX quote of 1.50 in the case of the British pound means 1.50 US dollars per British pound, or 1.50 $/£, which is the FX price of a British pound (in US dollars). Other significant currencies usually quoted in American terms include the euro (€), the Australian dollar (A$), and the New Zealand dollar (Z$).

From a country's perspective, an FX rate is said to be in *direct terms* if the home currency is the pricing currency and in *indirect terms* if the foreign currency is the pricing currency. Thus, the FX rate of 2 $/£ is in direct terms from the U.S. point of view and indirect terms from the British point of view, because the US dollar is the pricing currency, that is, in the numerator. The FX rate of 0.50 £/$ is in indirect terms from the U.S. point of view, but is in direct terms from the British point of view.

An FX rate for immediate delivery is called a *spot FX rate*. The notation for a spot FX rate in this text is the capital letter X. To keep things straight, generally we'll follow X with a two-currency superscript. Thus, $X^{Sfr/\$}$ represents a spot FX rate expressed in Swiss francs per US dollar. $X^{\$/£}$ would represent a spot FX rate expressed in US dollars per British pound. We'll often use a subscript to denote time. Thus $X_0^{\$/£}$ denotes a current spot FX rate, $X_1^{\$/£}$ is the spot FX rate at time 1, $X_N^{\$/£}$ is the spot FX rate at time N, and so forth.

To compute the percentage change in the spot FX price of a currency, you use FX rates expressed with that currency in the denominator. The percentage change in the spot FX price of the euro versus the US dollar, over the period from time 0 to time N, is denoted as $x_N^{\$/€}$, and is equal to $(X_N^{\$/€} - X_0^{\$/€})/X_0^{\$/€}$. (The text often uses *lower case letters* to denote percentage-change variables.) A shortcut for this calculation that we'll frequently use is shown in equation (1):

Percentage FX Change: Euro versus US Dollar

$$x_N^{\$/€} = X_N^{\$/€}/X_0^{\$/€} - 1 \qquad (1)$$

For example, if the euro depreciates versus the US dollar from 1.25 $/€ to 1 $/€, the percentage change in the euro versus the US dollar is (1 $/€)/(1.25 $/€) – 1 = –0.20, or –20%.

To compute a currency's percentage change when the currency is the "numerator" of the FX rate quote, you need think in terms of reciprocal FX rates. For example, if the FX rate for the yen goes from 100 ¥/$ to 80 ¥/$, the percentage change in the yen is not –20%; instead, it is the US dollar that changes by –20% versus the yen. The FX price of the yen changes from 0.01 $/¥ to 0.0125 $/¥, a percentage change of (0.0125 $/¥)/(0.01 $/¥) – 1 = 0.25, or a 25% appreciation of the yen versus the US dollar. The relationship between the percentage FX changes from the two currency directions in equation (2) may come in handy:

Percentage FX Change and Currency Direction

$$(1 + x^{S/¥}) (1 + x^{¥/S}) = 1 \qquad (2)$$

Thus, per equation (2), a 20% depreciation of the US dollar versus the yen implies a percentage change in the yen versus the US dollar of $1/(1 - 0.20) - 1 = 0.25$, or 25%.

Assume that the spot FX rate for the Swiss franc goes from 1.50 Sf/$ to 1.25 Sf/$. (a) Find the percentage change in the FX price of the US dollar versus the Swiss franc, and state whether this change is an appreciation or depreciation of the US dollar. (b) Find the percentage change in the FX price of the Swiss franc versus the US dollar, and state whether the change is an appreciation or a depreciation of the Swiss franc. (c) Verify equation (2).

Answers: (a) The percentage change in the FX price of the US dollar versus the Swiss franc is $x^{Sf/S} = (1.25\ Sf/\$)/(1.50\ Sf/\$) - 1 = -0.1667$, or –16.67%. Thus, the US dollar depreciates by 16.67% versus the Swiss franc. (b) Reciprocating the FX rates directly in equation (1), we have $x^{S/Sf} = [1/(1.25\ Sf/\$)]/[1/(1.50\ Sf/\$)] - 1 = 0.20$, or a 20% appreciation of the Swiss franc versus the US dollar. (c) $(1 - 0.1667)(1 + 0.20) = 1$.

CHAPTER 1

Global Risk and Return

As the future value of an investment is usually uncertain, an investor needs to think in terms of an *expected* rate of return. The investor has a target expected rate of return that will compensate for the risk specific to the investment. That target expected rate of return is sometimes called the *required rate of return* for the investment. Given the risk taken, an investor makes a sound investment if the <u>actual</u> expected rate of return exceeds the <u>required</u> rate of return.

Finance models are often cast in terms of an investment's aggregate required rate of return, meaning the "market's" required rate of return. This is sometimes called the *opportunity cost of capital*, or simply the investment's *cost of capital*. Another synonym is the *equilibrium expected rate of return*, which is the expected rate of return only if the investment is correctly priced in the market.

An important question is which risk–return model is best to use to determine how an investment's cost of capital should be traded off against the investment's risk. A long-standing risk–return model is the traditional *Capital Asset Pricing Model* (*CAPM*), which is covered in many finance courses and used extensively by practitioners.

In this chapter and the next, we extend the CAPM to internationally integrated financial markets. Given the significant extent of real-world financial market integration and international diversification, an international risk–return model seems logically superior to the traditional CAPM, which is usually applied as a local (or domestic) risk–return model.

This chapter introduces the simple *global CAPM* (*GCAPM*), which looks like the traditional CAPM except that the global market index replaces the domestic market index. The *international CAPM* (*ICAPM*) is more complex but theoretically stronger than the GCAPM. The next chapter introduces a version of the ICAPM that has some benefits that may justify the additional complexity.

In some currencies, including the US dollar, the simpler GCAPM provides an acceptable approximation to the more complex ICAPM estimate of an asset's cost of capital. However, the GCAPM may <u>not</u> give an acceptable approximation to the ICAPM when estimating cost of capital in some other currencies or when estimating currency risk premiums.

Traditional CAPM Review

The traditional CAPM is a widely used risk–return model: In a 2012 survey of 19 highly regarded U.S. companies, all but one reported using the CAPM to estimate cost of capital. The CAPM continues to be controversial in academic circles, but remains the primary risk–return model in finance textbooks. A 2009 survey of finance professors found that 75% recommend the CAPM approach to the cost of capital.[1]

The well-known traditional CAPM equation is $k_i = r_f + \beta_i[MRP]$, where k_i is asset i's cost of capital; r_f is the risk-free rate of return; β_i is asset i's risk measure (called "beta"); and MRP denotes the market risk premium, which is the risk premium required on the market index by the representative investor. We next elaborate on all four of these variables.

The k_i variable is also called asset i's *equilibrium* expected rate of return, which is only equal to the *actual* expected asset return if the asset is correctly priced in the market.

A standard practice in U.S. applications has been to use a U.S. Treasury yield for r_f. Historically, there has been disagreement on whether to use a short-term or long-term rate. Recent survey evidence shows that managers strongly prefer using a long-term rate.[2]

The "beta" risk measure, β_i, is asset i's sensitivity to unexpected returns on the market index. If an asset has a beta of 1.20 and the market index's rate of return is 10% higher than expected, then the asset's rate of return will tend to be (on average) 1.20(10%) = 12% higher than expected. The beta of the market index is 1, by definition.

The market risk premium, MRP, is equal to $k_M - r_f$, which is the required rate of return on the market index minus the risk-free rate;

$k_M - r_f$ is the compensation for the risk in the diversified portfolio represented by the market index, and is properly named the *MRP*. As with individual assets, the difference between the market index's *actual* expected rate of return and the risk-free rate is not truly a risk premium because the market index's possible misvaluation is incorporated.

In the traditional CAPM, the *market price of risk* is the *MRP* divided by the variance of market index returns, where the variance measures aggregate market risk. The market price of risk is driven by the average investor's degree of risk aversion. Thus, the *MRP* tends to change as overall market volatility changes and as investors' tolerance for risk fluctuates with economic conditions.

Years ago, it was standard to use a range of 7% to 9% for the U.S. *MRP*. More recent estimates for the U.S. *MRP* tend to be in the range of 4% to 7%.[3] Exhibit 1.1 shows some U.S. market risk premium estimates over recent years, which are from Aswath Damodaran's website. The average of the *MRP* estimates is 5.65%.

Given the modern range of 4% to 7%, reasonable estimates of the U.S. *MRP* are: In a "normal" market period, use an estimate in the 5%

Exhibit 1.1 U.S. market risk premium (MRP) estimates

2002	4.73%
2003	4.74%
2004	4.86%
2005	5.22%
2006	6.12%
2007	4.59%
2008	6.92%
2009	4.64%
2010	6.09%
2011	8.34%
2012	7.30%
2013	4.99%
2014	5.38%
2015	5.16%

Source: Damodaran: http://pages.stern.nyu.edu/~adamodar/

to 6% range. If the market is relatively depressed due to heightened risk aversion ("fear"), use an *MRP* estimate in the 6% to 7% range. And if the market is in an aggressive stage with higher tolerance for risk ("greed"), use an estimate in the 4% to 5% range.

Rate of Return on a Foreign Asset

We first address the notion of a given asset's rate of return in different currencies. Specifically, an asset's rate of return in one currency depends on the rate of return in another currency and the change in the spot FX rate between the two currencies, as shown in equation (1.1a). Equation (1.1a) shows the conversion of asset i's rate of return in euros, $R_i^{\euro}$, to the same asset's rate of return in US dollars, $R_i^{\$}$, using the percentage change in the FX price of the euro (in US dollars), $x^{\$/\euro}$.

Asset's Rate of Return in Different Currencies

$$1 + R_i^{\$} = \left(1 + R_i^{\euro}\right)\left(1 + x^{\$/\euro}\right) \qquad (1.1a)$$

For example, if an asset's rate of return in euros is 20%, and the euro appreciates by 5% versus the US dollar, the same asset's rate of return in US dollars is $(1.20)(1.05) - 1 = 0.26$, or 26%.

The rate of return in British pounds on a share of stock on the London Stock Exchange is 15%. During the same period, the British pound depreciates by 8% versus the US dollar. Find the rate of return on the stock from the US dollar perspective.

Answer: $(1.15)(1 - 0.08) - 1 = 0.058$, or 5.8%.

A NASDAQ stock's rate of return in US dollars is 15%. During the same period, the British pound depreciates by 8% versus the US dollar. Find the stock's rate of return from the British pound perspective.

Answer: $(1.15)/(1 - 0.08) - 1 = 0.25$, or 25%.

If you multiply the right-hand side of equation (1.1a), you get that $R_i^\$ = R_i^\mathcal{E} + x^{\$/\mathcal{E}} + R_i^\mathcal{E} x^{\$/\mathcal{E}}$. For purposes of simplification, the cross-product term is sometimes ignored to have a linear approximation. Thus, an often-used linear approximation to equation (1.1a) is given in equation (1.1b).

Asset's Rate of Return: Different Currencies

Linear Approximation

$$R_i^\$ \approx R_i^\mathcal{E} + x^{\$/\mathcal{E}} \qquad (1.1b)$$

Global CAPM

There is a tendency to think in terms of a separate CAPM for each country: a CAPM in US dollars for U.S. investments, a CAPM in British pounds for U.K. investments, and so forth. This tendency is partly natural and partly based on the not-so-distant past when national financial markets were relatively segmented from each other. But this tendency is a mistake now that the world's financial markets are substantially integrated. Now we need to think in terms of a <u>common</u> risk–return trade-off for assets in the internationally integrated financial markets, regardless of asset nationality or whether we choose to express the trade-off in US dollars, in British pounds, or in any other currency.

We now introduce the global CAPM, or GCAPM, in which the market index is the *global market index*. The global market index is sometimes also called the world market index, but technically the global market index contains only globally accessible assets, whereas the world market index also contains assets that are restricted from international portfolios.[4] Exhibit 1.2 shows some equity capitalization percentages of the global equity market index (2005).

It is important to see that the composition of the global market index is the same for all investors in the market, regardless of nationality or currency. That is, even though the global market index includes assets from different countries, the index's composition is the same regardless of which currency we choose to express the index's return. Just as the rate of return on any asset in the world may be converted between currencies by equation (1.1a), the rate of return on any portfolio of assets, including

Exhibit 1.2 Global equity capitalization: Major market percentages (2005)

United States	55%
Eurozone	14%
United Kingdom	11%
Japan	11%
Canada	4%
Switzerland	3%
Australia	3%

Source: Campbell, Serfaty-de Medeiros, and Viceira (2010).

the global market index, may be expressed in terms of any currency. Many think the best global market index is the MSCI ACWI (All Country World Index), where MSCI stands for Morgan Stanley Capital International.

One concern about using a CAPM with a global market index is that real-world investors have tended to invest more in assets of their own country than would be advisable, given the benefits of international diversification. This tendency is called *home bias*. Researchers have been studying home bias, and debating whether it means that local, country-specific CAPMs still have some relevance. At the same time, researchers have also found that home bias has been diminishing. The extent of investors' international diversification and financial market integration suggests that a global market index is a more appropriate benchmark in internationally integrated financial markets than a traditional local market index.

The GCAPM risk–return relation is the same as the traditional CAPM except that the global market index replaces the local (domestic) market index. Equation (1.2) shows the GCAPM risk–return trade-off formula:

Global CAPM (GCAPM)

$$k_i^C = r_f^C + \beta_{iG}^C \left[GRP^C \right] \tag{1.2}$$

In equation (1.2), k_i^C is asset i's required rate of return, or cost of capital, from the perspective of currency C. The beta, β_{iG}^C, is the asset's *global beta*, measured using returns in currency C. This beta measures the sensitivity of asset i's return, adjusted into currency C if a foreign asset, relative to the return in currency C of the global market index. GRP^C represents the required risk premium for the global market index, or *global risk premium*, from the perspective of currency C, which is the equilibrium expected rate of return (or required rate of return) on the global market index in currency C minus the currency-C risk-free rate, r_f^C.

The rate of return conversion formula in equation (1.1a) should make it clear that an asset's global beta and required rate of return expressed in one currency are not the same numbers when expressed in a different currency. For example, the global equity beta estimate for United Technologies Corporation (using 1999 to 2016 data) was 0.94; converting the returns to euros results in a global beta estimate in euros of 0.99. Therefore, we use the superscript symbol to denote that the variables are from the perspective of currency C.

Since the average U.S. market risk premium estimate in Exhibit 1.1 is 5.65%, and the U.S. market index's beta estimate (versus the global market index) was about 0.94 using 1999 to 2016 data, we use equation (1.2) to infer that an average global market risk premium in US dollars ($GRP^\$$) has been approximately 5.65%/0.94 = 6%. For convenience in examples, we will frequently use a global risk premium in US dollars of 6%.

Figure 1.1 shows a diagram for the GCAPM in US dollars. The line is the relationship between risk and expected return in US dollars for assets in the global financial market that are correctly priced (i.e., in equilibrium) in US dollars. The slope of the line is the $GRP^\$$, assumed in the diagram to be 6%. The risk–return line intercepts the Y-axis at the US dollar risk-free rate, assumed in the diagram to be 3%.

Using the GCAPM to estimate an asset's required rate of return is procedurally the same as using the traditional CAPM. Assume that the US dollar risk-free rate is 3% and the global risk premium in US dollars is 6%. Given asset i's global beta estimate in US dollars is 1.20, asset i's cost of capital estimate in US dollars is $k_i^\$ = 0.03 + 1.20[0.06] = 0.102$, or 10.2%.

Assume General Electric's global equity beta (in US dollars) is 0.69; the US dollar risk-free rate is 3%; and the global risk premium in US dollars is 6%. Find GE's cost of equity in US dollars with the GCAPM.

Answer: 0.03 + 0.69[0.06] = 0.0714, or 7.14%.

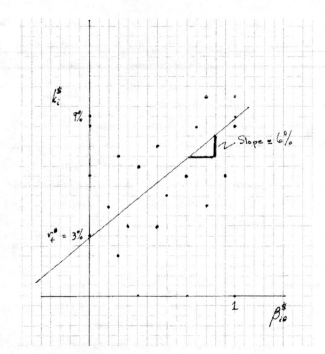

Figure 1.1 Global CAPM (GCAPM) in US dollars

If an asset is correctly valued in US dollars, its expected return and beta will plot exactly on the equilibrium risk–return line. If an asset is undervalued (overvalued), its actual expected return will plot above (below) what the line says the expected return should be for the risk. Misvalued assets are represented as scatter dots off the risk–return line in Figure 1.1. In US dollars, a foreign asset can be misvalued for either of two reasons: (a) the asset is misvalued in its own currency; or (b) the spot FX rate is misvalued. Therefore, the global market index may, in principle, be sometimes misvalued due to an FX misvaluation of foreign stocks in the global market index. Thus, even the global market index can be misvalued and plot off the equilibrium risk–return line.

GCAPM Versus Local CAPM

There are currently no published global equity beta estimates like there are for traditional equity betas (versus a domestic index) at online financial services. Now, the only way to get a stock's global beta estimate is to do a

Exhibit 1.3 Global and local beta estimates (in US dollars). Selected U.S. equities

COMPANY	$\beta_{iG}^{\$}$	$\beta_{iL}^{\$}$
EXXON	0.85	0.73
GENERAL ELECTRIC	0.69	0.81
IBM	1.03	1.19
MERCK	0.54	0.63
MICROSOFT	0.85	0.97

Source: Author's calculations with monthly rates of return, 2002–2007.

regression analysis using historical return observations, which is easy on Bloomberg. Exhibit 1.3's $\beta_{iG}^{\$}$ column shows global equity beta estimates against the MSCI ACWI for a few selected U.S. stocks. The estimated traditional equity betas, called *local betas*, are shown in the $\beta_{iL}^{\$}$ column for comparison.

Whether a stock's global beta is higher or lower than its traditional local beta depends on the drivers of the stock's returns relative to domestic and international economic conditions. For example, IBM's global equity beta estimate in US dollars is 1.03 in Exhibit 1.3. This estimate represents the systematic risk of the firm's equity shares in a globally diversified portfolio. IBM's traditional local beta estimate for the same period is 1.19. This estimate is for IBM equity's systematic risk in a diversified portfolio of U.S. stocks only. So, IBM's stock contributes less risk to a diversified global portfolio than to a diversified domestic U.S. portfolio. On the other hand, Exxon's global beta estimate is higher than the local beta estimate, per Exhibit 1.3. Exxon's stock contributes relatively more risk to a diversified global portfolio than to a diversified U.S. domestic portfolio.

It is important to see that the GCAPM typically gives a different cost of equity estimate than the traditional local CAPM. For example, assume the US dollar risk-free rate is 3% and the global risk premium in US dollars is 6%. With IBM's global beta of 1.03, the estimated US dollar cost of equity for IBM with the GCAPM is 0.03 + 1.03[0.06] = 0.0918, or 9.18%. Using 5.65% for the local U.S. market risk premium, IBM's estimated cost of equity with the traditional local U.S. CAPM would be 0.03 + 1.19[0.0565] = 0.0972, or 9.72%.

Use the estimates for General Electric's global equity beta (in US dollars) and local U.S. equity beta from Exhibit 1.3. Assume that the US dollar risk-free rate is 3%, the global risk premium in US dollars is 6%, and the U.S. market risk premium is 5.65%. (a) Estimate GE's cost of equity in US dollars with the GCAPM. (b) Compare this estimate with the one for the traditional local U.S. CAPM.

Answers: (a) GE's estimated global equity beta is 0.69. For the GCAPM, GE's cost of equity estimate in US dollars is 0.03 + 0.69[0.06] = 0.0714, or 7.14%. (b) GE's estimated local US equity beta is 0.81. Using the local U.S. CAPM, GE's cost of equity estimate in US dollars is 0.03 + 0.81[0.0565] = 0.0758, or 7.58%.

The IBM and GE examples show that the GCAPM and the traditional local CAPM do not give the same cost of equity estimates. The differences are partly due to the differences between the local and global market risk premium estimates (5.65% vs. 6% in the examples here), and partly due to differences in local and global betas.

A recent study found an average absolute difference of over 90 basis points between GCAPM and traditional local CAPM cost of equity estimates for many U.S. equities for the 1985 to 2012 period. For firms with high (positive or negative) FX equity exposure estimates, the average difference was almost 150 basis points.[5]

American Depositary Receipts (ADRs) and Dual-Listed Shares

American Depositary Receipts (ADRs) are foreign equity shares directly traded in the United States in US dollars. The foreign office of a depositary, such as Bank of New York Mellon, will hold the actual foreign shares in that foreign country, while the bank's U.S. office issues US dollar-denominated receipts that are more easily traded in U.S. markets. Stocks traded on both home and foreign exchanges are said to be *cross-listed stocks*.

The first ADR was offered by JP Morgan in 1927. In 1990, there were only 352 non-U.S. stocks traded on the New York Stock Exchange

(NYSE) and NASDAQ. By the end of 2002, the number was more than 850. If one includes over-the-counter and private placement issues, there are now more than 4,300 foreign companies, from 84 countries, with shares traded in the United States. This development reflects the U.S. investors' appetite for international diversification and the desire of foreign companies to access global capital, broaden their shareholder base, and enhance company visibility. Widely held ADRs include: Vodaphone (U.K.), Baidu (China), Royal Dutch Shell (U.K.), Daimler AG (Germany), and Novartis (Switzerland).

The price of an ADR should, in principle, obey the "international law of one price," or there will be a relatively easy arbitrage opportunity between the ADR shares and the actual underlying shares, called the *ordinary shares*. If the ordinary shares of Siemens are priced in Germany at €100 per share at time 0, when the spot FX rate is 1.25 $/€, then the ADRs should be priced at $125 per share in the United States. Otherwise, there would be a relatively easy arbitrage opportunity for traders who have access to both markets. The same reasoning tells us that if the ordinary Siemens shares are priced in Germany at €120 per share at time 1, when the spot FX rate is 1.50 $/€, the ADR price in the United States should be $180 per share. In reality, some pricing differences have been observed in between ADRs and the ordinaries.[6]

Given no arbitrage opportunity between Siemens ADRs and the ordinaries, an investor in the ADRs would earn the same rate of return in US dollars as an investor in the ordinaries: $180/$125 − 1 = 0.44, or 44%. This rate of return is consistent with equation (1.1a): Since the rate of return on Siemens ordinaries in euros is 20% and the euro appreciates by 20%, equation (1.1a) says that the return in US dollars is $(1.20)(1.20) − 1 = 0.44$. Ignoring transaction costs and other frictions, there is no difference in whether a U.S. investor holds the actual Siemens ordinary shares or the ADRs. The rate of return in US dollars is the same, as the ADR returns will reflect both returns on an ordinary share and changes in the spot FX rate.

ADRs often trade in a share ratio different from one-for-one. For example, one ADR for Telefonos de Mexico represents 20 underlying Mexican shares, while one ADR for Diageo (a British company that resulted from the merger of Guinness and Grand Metropolitan in 1997) represents four ordinary U.K. shares.

The ordinary shares for Diageo are denominated in British pounds and traded on the London Stock Exchange (LSE). There is one ADR share for every four ordinary shares. At time 0, the price of an ordinary share is £10 in London and the spot FX rate is 2 $/£. At time 1, the ordinary shares are priced at £12 and the spot FX rate is 1.60 $/£. (a) Find the no-arbitrage price of a Diageo ADR share at time 0. (b) Find the time-1 no-arbitrage price of an ADR share. (c) Find the rate of return to a U.S. investor who buys the Diageo ordinary shares at time 0 and holds until time 1.

Answers: (a) An ordinary share is worth £10(2 $/£) = $20 at time 0. Since 4 ordinary shares underlie 1 ADR share, an ADR share should be priced at 4($20) = $80 at time 0. (b) An ordinary share is worth £12(1.60 $/£) = $19.20 at time 1. An ADR share should be priced at 4($19.20) = $76.80 at time 1. (c) Thus, the rate of return in US dollars is $76.80/80 − 1 = −0.04, or −4%.

The proportion of U.S. trading (in ADRs) of a foreign company's shares varies. Tomkins, a U.K. engineering company has relatively little U.S. trading, but GlaxoSmithKline, a U.K. pharmaceutical company, experiences U.S. trading of about 30%. The larger the percentage of trading in the United States, the more the price is determined in the U.S. market instead of the home market. But in principle, the no-arbitrage relationship should hold regardless of the primary market of price determination.[7]

In contrast to ADRs, "law of one price" violations have been more regularly observed for *dual-listed shares*. In a dual-listed shares arrangement, separate but related companies in different countries pay a combined cash flow to the shareholders of the companies. One company's shares are not convertible into the other's, but both shares are claims on equivalent cash flow streams.

BHP Billiton is one example of a company with dual-listed shares. BHP Billiton's shares are held by two separate entities, BHP Billiton Ltd in Australia and BHP Billiton Plc in the United Kingdom. BHP Billiton Ltd's shares trade in Australia in Australian dollars and have a widely held ADR in the United States, and BHP Billiton Plc's shares trade in the United Kingdom in British pounds and also have a widely held ADR in the United States. Other companies with dual-listed shares include Investec (South Africa); Mondi (South Africa/UK), Reed Elsevier (UK/Netherlands), Rio Tinto Group (Australia/UK), and Unilever (UK/Netherlands).

In perfect international financial markets in which there are no taxes, restrictions, or other "frictions," dual-listed shares should sell at equivalent prices, given the spot FX rate. However, researchers have found deviations from pricing parity in dual-listed shares because the existence of various "frictions" makes perfect, easy arbitrage impossible. These pricing deviations are like those observed between Chinese A-shares and B-shares, where A-shares may only be held by Chinese investors, whereas B-shares may only be owned by non-Chinese investors.[8]

ADRs and dual-listed shares help us see why it is generally incorrect to use country-specific local CAPMs in a world of internationally integrated financial markets. Say we try to estimate Sony's cost of equity, both in yen using a local Japan CAPM with an estimate of Sony's traditional equity beta against a Japanese market index (in yen), and in US dollars using the traditional local U.S. CAPM with an estimate of Sony's ADR beta against a U.S. market index. The mistake with this method is that nothing ensures the no-arbitrage pricing link between the Sony ordinary shares and the Sony ADRs. Sony's ordinary shares are effectively the same asset as the ADRs, but with a different currency denomination; this fact implies that the cost of equity from the different currency perspectives should be based on the asset's systematic risk relative to the same market factor (or factors), but from the different currency perspectives. The GCAPM is based on the idea that in internationally integrated financial markets, assets should be valued using a common risk-return model. Therefore, it would be theoretically more correct to use the GCAPM for both estimations, using Sony's global equity beta and the global market index from the yen perspective to estimate Sony's cost of equity in yen, and using the global beta and global market index from the US dollar perspective to estimate Sony's equity (ADR) beta in US dollars.

It turns out, however, that although the GCAPM may be an OK cost of capital model for the US dollar perspective, the GCAPM may not be as useful from some other currency perspectives, as we'll explain in the next chapter using a version of the theoretically superior global risk–return model called the *international CAPM (ICAPM)*.

Summary Action Points

- In international finance theory, all assets should obey an equilibrium risk–return relation from the perspective of a given currency, regardless of the assets' nationalities/home currencies.
- The global CAPM (GCAPM) is similar in form to the traditional CAPM, but the market index is a global market index. An asset's global beta tends to be different from its local beta.
- In principle, there is a no-arbitrage relation between the price of an American Depositary Receipt (ADR), the home currency price of the underlying ordinary share, and the spot FX rate.

Glossary

American Depositary Receipts (ADRs): U.S. dollar-denominated and U.S. market-traded receipts on foreign-issued shares.

Beta: The sensitivity of an asset's rate of return relative to the overall market, which is the asset's systematic risk.

Cost of Equity: The equilibrium expected rate of return as compensation for risk of an equity investment.

Cross-listed Stocks: Stocks traded on both their home and foreign exchanges.

Dual-listed Shares: An arrangement where separate, but related companies in different countries pay a combined cash flow to the shareholders of the companies.

Global CAPM (GCAPM): A simple model of risk and return in internationally integrated financial markets in which the global market index replaces the traditional CAPM market index.

Global Beta: The beta of an asset's rate of return versus the global market index, measuring the tendency of the asset's returns to change systematically with the returns of the global market index.

Global Risk Premium: The minimum rate of return over the risk-free rate that investors (in the aggregate) require as compensation for risk in the global market index.

Home Bias: The tendency of investors to invest more in stocks of their own country than would be advisable given the benefits of international diversification.

Local Beta: The beta of an asset's rate of return versus the local (domestic) market index, measuring the tendency of the returns to change systematically with the returns of the local market index.

Market Risk Premium: The minimum rate of return over the risk-free rate that investors (in the aggregate) require as compensation for the risk in the market index.

Ordinary Shares or Ordinaries: The actual local market shares that underlie depositary receipts trading in another market.

Required Rate of Return: The expected rate of return required as compensation for investing capital and bearing risk.

Problems

1. The rate of return in Swiss francs on a share of stock on the Swiss Stock Exchange is 15%. During the same period, the spot FX rate changes from 1 Sf/$ to 1.25 Sf/$. What is the rate of return on the stock from the US dollar perspective?
2. The rate of return in Swiss francs on a share of stock on the Swiss Stock Exchange is –15%. During the same period, the spot FX rate changes from 1 Sf/$ to 1.20 Sf/$. What is the rate of return on the stock from the US dollar perspective?
3. The rate of return in US dollars on a share of stock on the New York Stock Exchange is 15%. During the same period, the spot FX rate changes from 1 Sf/$ to 1.25 Sf/$. What is the rate of return on the stock from the Swiss franc perspective?
4. Brown & Co.'s global equity beta in US dollars is 1.25. Estimate the cost of equity in US dollars using the GCAPM, given a US dollar risk-free rate of 3% and a global risk premium of 6% in US dollars.

5. Assume the U.S. equity market index has a global beta in US dollars of 1. With the GCAPM, what is the US equity market risk premium, given a US dollar risk-free rate of 3% and a global risk premium of 6% in US dollars?

6. Sony's ADR shares are traded on the New York Stock Exchange. There is one ADR share of Sony for each ordinary share. (a) If the ordinary shares are priced at ¥3,750 in Tokyo, and if the spot FX rate is 110 ¥/$, find the no-arbitrage price of a Sony ADR share in US dollars. (b) Find the time-1 price of a Sony ADR share when the ordinary shares are priced at ¥4,375 and the spot FX rate is 125 ¥/$?

7. Use information from the previous problem. Find the rate of return to a U.S. investor who buys Sony ADRs at time 0 and holds until time 1.

8. Sony's ADR shares are traded on the New York Stock Exchange. There is one ADR share of Sony for each ordinary Tokyo share. At time 0, the ordinary shares are priced at ¥4,000 in Tokyo, and the spot FX rate is 80 ¥/$. At time 1, the ordinary shares are priced at ¥5,000 in Tokyo, and the spot FX rate is 100 ¥/$. If there is no arbitrage possible between the Sony ADR shares and the ordinary shares, find the rate of return to a U.S. investor who buys Sony ADRs at time 0 and holds until time 1.

9. CSN (Companhia Siderurgica Nacional, a real company) is a Brazilian steel products company with ordinary shares traded in Brazilian real in Sao Paulo and ADRs traded on the NYSE in US dollars. One ADR is equivalent to one ordinary share. The ordinary share price is currently Re 60 per share. The spot FX rate is 1.60 Re/$. (a) Find the no-arbitrage price in US dollars of an ADR share. (b) If an ordinary share's rate of return over the next year is −20%, and the Brazilian real appreciates by 10% versus the US dollar, find the rate of return on an ADR share in US dollars.

Answers to Problems

1. The US dollar appreciates by 25% versus the Swissie, so the Swissie depreciates by 20% versus the US dollar. The rate of return on the stock in US dollars is $(1.15)(1 − 0.20) − 1 = −0.08$, or −8%.

2. Approximately: −15% − 16.67% = −31.67%; Exactly: (1 − 0.15) (1 − 0.1667) − 1 = −0.29, or −29%.

3. (1.15)(1 + 0.25) − 1 = 0.4375, or 43.75%.

4. Using the GCAPM, 0.03 + 1.25[0.06] = 0.105, or 10.5%.

5. Same as global risk premium, 6%.

6. (a) An ADR share is worth ¥3,750/(110 ¥/$) = $34.09.

   (b) The new ADR share price will be ¥4,375/(125 ¥/$) = $35.

7. The rate of return in US dollars = $35/34.09 − 1 = 0.0267, or 2.67%.

8. $50/$50 − 1 = 0.

9. (a) Re 60/(1.60 Re/$) = $37.50;

10. (b) 0.80(1.10) − 1 = −0.12, or −12%.

Discussion Questions

1. Discuss the pros and cons of using the GCAPM to estimate a firm's cost of equity.

2. The actual expected rate of return on the market index is 12% and the risk-free rate is 3%. The market is undervalued. Should you use 9% as the market risk premium in the CAPM? Explain.

3. Why should a foreign stock be in the same risk–return equilibrium as U.S. stocks?

CHAPTER 2

The International CAPM

Although the global CAPM (GCAPM) is the simplest risk and return model for internationally integrated financial markets, the GCAPM is not always the best model to use. You will see in this chapter that the GCAPM is a reasonable risk–return model from the US dollar perspective and perhaps from the perspective of a few other currencies as well. For many other currencies, on the other hand, one may want to apply instead the version of the *international CAPM* (*ICAPM*) introduced in this chapter.

Introduction to the Two-Factor ICAPM

Whereas the local CAPM and the GCAPM each have only one risk factor, the ICAPM version introduced in the following has two risk factors: (1) the global market index; and (2) a foreign currency index, constructed as described in the box. Because of the two risk factors, an asset has two measures of systematic risk in the ICAPM. An asset has both a "beta," which measures sensitivity to the global market index, and a "gamma," which measures sensitivity to the foreign currency index. The "gamma" risk coefficient (γ) is called the asset's *FX exposure* (to the foreign currency index).[1]

The ICAPM thus involves two-factor risk premiums from the perspective of home currency H: (1) the global risk premium, GRP^H, which is the required rate of return on the global market index in currency H minus the currency-H risk-free rate, $k_G^H - r_f^H$; and (2) the foreign currency index risk premium, XRP^H, which is the risk premium of the foreign currency index, from the perspective of currency H, $k_X^H - r_f^H$, where k_X^H is the required return on the foreign currency index, inclusive of FX changes and foreign currency risk-free rates.

Each of the two ICAPM factor risk premiums is the sum of two components: (1) $GRP^H = GRP_1^H + GRP_2^H$; and (2) $XRP^H = XRP_1^H + XRP_2^H$.

ICAPM Foreign Currency Index

From the perspective of the home currency H, the foreign currency index contains a position in each of the other currencies. Each position in the foreign currency index is a risk-free, interest-earning deposit in currency C, and has a return equal to the percentage change in currency C versus currency H, $x^{H/C}$, plus the currency-C risk-free rate. The weights on the index's currency deposit positions are based on national financial wealth, which is not necessarily the same as an economy's percentage of global equity market capitalization.

The world wealth percentages for the 21 economies listed in Exhibit 2.1, from the *Credit Suisse Research Institute Global Wealth Databook* for 2015, represent 94% of world wealth. Exhibit 2.1 shows the wealth weight estimates, w_C, which are the 21 world wealth percentages normalized to sum to 100%.

The composition of the foreign currency index is different for each different home currency perspective, because the index contains currencies that are foreign from the perspective of currency H. The position weight for currency C in currency-H's foreign currency index is w_C divided by $(1 - w_H)$. For example, the euro's weight in the US dollar's foreign currency index is $0.204/(1 - 0.379) = 0.329$, or 32.9%. The US dollar's weight in the euro's foreign currency index is $0.379/(1 - 0.204) = 0.476$, or 47.6%.

The first GRP^H component accounts for the risk in the global market index from the currency-H perspective and the aggregate market's degree of aversion to that risk: $GRP_1^H = \Theta\left[(\sigma_G^H)^2\right]$, where Θ denotes the global market price of risk, and σ_G^H is the volatility (standard deviation) of the global market index return from the perspective of currency H. GRP_1^H is the same as the global risk premium would be if the GCAPM held in currency H, or if there were no correlation between the returns on the global market index and the foreign currency index from the perspective of currency H. The second GRP^H component is: $GRP_2^H = (1 - \Theta)\left[\gamma_G^H(1 - w_H)(\sigma_X^H)^2\right]$, where γ_G^H **is the FX exposure of the global market index to the foreign currency index**, which accounts for the systematic risk of the global market index versus the foreign currency index; w_H is the wealth weight of the currency-H economy; and σ_X^H is the volatility of the foreign currency index return.[2]

For example, assume $\Theta = 2.50$ and the following inputs (shown in Exhibit 2.1) for the US dollar perspective: $w_s = 0.379$; $\sigma_G^\$ = 0.1594$; $\sigma_X^\$ = 0.0616$; and $\gamma_G^\$ = 1.23$. The two GRP^H components are: $GRP_1^\$ = 2.50[(0.1594)^2] = 0.0635$; and $GRP_2^\$ = (1 - 2.50)[1.23(1 - 0.379)(0.0616)^2] = -0.0043$, or -0.43%. Adding the components, we get the **global risk premium in US dollars**: $GRP^\$ = 0.0635 - 0.0043 = 0.0592$, or **5.92%**.

ICAPM Factor Risk Premiums

Global Risk Premium

$$GRP^H = GRP_1^H + GRP_2^H$$

$$GRP_1^H = \Theta\left[\left(\sigma_G^H\right)^2\right]$$

$$GRP_2^H = (1-\Theta)\left[\gamma_G^H\left(1-w_H\right)\left(\sigma_X^H\right)^2\right]$$

Foreign Currency Index Risk Premium

$$XRP^H = XRP_1^H + XRP_2^H$$

$$XRP_1^H = (1-\Theta)\left[\left(1-w_H\right)\left(\sigma_X^H\right)^2\right]$$

$$XRP_2^H = \Theta\left[\beta_X^H\left(\sigma_G^H\right)^2\right]$$

Θ = Market Price of Risk

σ_G^H = Volatility of Global Market Index Return

σ_X^H = Volatility of Foreign Currency Index Return

γ_G^H = FX Exposure of Global Market Index versus the Foreign Currency Index

β_X^H = Foreign Currency Index's Global Beta

w_H = Wealth Weight of the Currency-H Economy

For the foreign currency index risk premium, XRP^H, the first component depends on the volatility of the foreign currency index and the relative wealth weight for currency H: $XRP_1^H = (1 - \Theta)\left[(1 - w_H)(\sigma_X^H)^2\right]$. The foreign currency index premium would be XRP_1^H given a zero correlation between the returns of the global market and the foreign currency index from the perspective of currency H. The second XRP^H component accounts for any systematic risk of the foreign currency index versus the global market index, through the **foreign currency index's global beta,** β_X^H : $XRP_2^H = \Theta\left[\beta_X^H\left(\sigma_G^H\right)^2\right]$.

For example, assume the foreign currency index has a beta from the US dollar perspective of $\beta_X^\$ = 0.183$ (as shown in Exhibit 2.1). If the US dollar is the home currency, the estimates of the two components of the foreign currency index risk premium are: $XRP_1^\$ = (1 - 2.50)[(1 - 0.379)$ $(0.0616)^2] = -0.0035$, or -0.35%; and $XRP_2^\$ = 2.50[0.183(0.1594)^2] = 0.0116$, or 1.16%. Adding the components, the **foreign currency index risk premium for the US dollar perspective** is: $XRP^\$ = -0.0035 + 0.0116 = 0.0081$, or **0.81%**.

For 21 currency perspectives, Exhibit 2.1 shows the ICAPM statistical input estimates for the factor risk premium estimates, which are calculated with data for 1999 to 2016. Exhibit 2.2 shows the ICAPM's two-factor risk premia, GRP^C and XRP^C, and the two components of each factor risk premium. The estimates assume $\Theta = 2.50$. Note that in the ICAPM, the global market price of risk, Θ, is the same number from any currency perspective, because there is only one market price of risk in a globally integrated market.

Per Exhibit 2.1 for the Australian dollar perspective: $w_{A\$} = 0.02$; $\sigma_G^{A\$} = 0.119$; $\sigma_X^{A\$} = 0.106$. *The global market index's estimated FX exposure to the foreign currency index* $\left(\gamma_G^{A\$}\right)$ *is 0.15, and the foreign currency index's estimated global beta* $\left(\beta_X^{A\$}\right)$ *is 0.12. Verify the* $GRP^{A\$}$ *and* $XRP^{A\$}$ *estimates in Exhibit 2.2 assuming* $= 2.50$.

Answer: $GRP_1^{A\$} = 2.50[(0.119)^2] = 0.0354$, *and* $GRP_2^{A\$} = (1 - 2.50)$ $[0.15(1 - 0.02)(0.106)^2] = -0.0025$. *Therefore,* $GRP^{A\$} = 0.0354 - 0.0025 = 0.0329$, *or 3.29%.* $XRP_1^{A\$} = (1 - 2.50)[(1 - 0.02)(0.106)^2] = -0.0165$, *and* $XRP_2^{A\$} = 2.50[0.12(0.119)^2] = 0.0042$. *Therefore,* $XRP^{A\$} = -0.0165 + 0.0042 = -0.0123$, *or -1.23%.*

**Exhibit 2.1 ICAPM Statistical Parameter Estimates:
Global Market Index and Foreign Currency Index**

Global Market Price of Risk = 2.50					
Statistical Parameter Estimation Period: 1999–2016					
	w_C	σ_G^C	σ_x^C	γ_G^C	β_x^C
United States (dollar)	0.379	0.159	0.062	1.23	0.18
Eurozone (euro)	0.204	0.149	0.088	0.46	0.16
Japan (yen)	0.130	0.188	0.095	1.36	0.35
China (yuan)	0.070	0.158	0.042	1.67	0.12
Britain (pound)	0.066	0.150	0.069	0.58	0.13
Canada (dollar)	0.026	0.123	0.079	−0.04	−0.02
Australia (dollar)	0.020	0.119	0.106	0.15	0.12
Taiwan (dollar)	0.015	0.141	0.041	0.07	0.01
Switzerland (franc)	0.015	0.167	0.080	1.01	0.23
India (rupee)	0.013	0.138	0.066	0.20	0.04
Korea (won)	0.012	0.129	0.097	0.23	0.13
Brazil (real)	0.009	0.237	0.242	0.78	0.81
Mexico (peso)	0.009	0.126	0.092	0.13	0.07
Sweden (krona)	0.008	0.133	0.085	0.22	0.09
Hong Kong (dollar)	0.005	0.159	0.038	2.00	0.11
Norway (krone)	0.004	0.141	0.087	0.39	0.15
Denmark (krone)	0.004	0.149	0.069	0.57	0.12
New Zealand (dollar)	0.004	0.135	0.113	0.36	0.26
Singapore (dollar)	0.004	0.139	0.036	−0.23	−0.02
South Africa (rand)	0.003	0.164	0.153	0.57	0.50
Thailand (baht)	0.001	0.146	0.065	0.50	0.10

Note in the boxed example problem that for the Australian dollar perspective, the global risk premium estimate, 3.29%, is lower than in US dollars, 5.92%, and the foreign currency index risk premium estimate, −1.23%, is also substantially lower than the one for the US dollar perspective, 0.81%. You will better understand these differences as we explore the ICAPM further in this and subsequent chapters. You will also learn why the examples assume a global market price of risk, Θ, of 2.50.

Exhibit 2.2 ICAPM Risk Premium Estimates:
Global Market Index and Foreign Currency Index

Global Market Price of Risk = 2.50						
Statistical Parameter Estimation Period: 1999–2016						
	GRP_1^C	GRP_2^C	GRP^C	XRP_1^C	XRP_2^C	XRP^C
United States (dollar)	6.35%	–0.43%	5.92%	–0.35%	1.16%	0.81%
Eurozone (euro)	5.54%	–0.46%	5.12%	–0.92%	0.88%	–0.04%
Japan (yen)	8.84%	–1.60%	7.24%	–1.18%	3.09%	1.91%
China (yuan)	6.23%	–0.40%	5.83%	–0.24%	0.72%	0.48%
Britain (pound)	5.59%	–0.39%	5.20%	–0.71%	0.73%	0.02%
Canada (dollar)	3.78%	0.03%	3.81%	–0.92%	–0.06%	–0.98%
Australia (dollar)	3.54%	–0.25%	3.29%	–1.65%	0.42%	–1.23%
Taiwan (dollar)	4.94%	–0.01%	4.93%	–0.25%	0.03%	–0.22%
Switzerland (franc)	6.93%	–0.96%	5.97%	–0.95%	1.62%	0.67%
India (rupee)	4.74%	–0.12%	4.62%	–0.64%	0.21%	–0.43%
Korea (won)	4.14%	–0.33%	3.81%	–1.41%	0.55%	–0.86%
Brazil (real)	14.09%	–6.81%	7.28%	–8.69%	11.46%	2.77%
Mexico (peso)	3.97%	–0.17%	3.80%	–1.25%	0.28%	–0.97%
Sweden (krona)	4.42%	–0.24%	4.18%	–1.07%	0.40%	–0.67%
Hong Kong (dollar)	6.33%	–0.42%	5.91%	–0.21%	0.71%	0.50%
Norway (krone)	4.99%	–0.44%	4.55%	–1.13%	0.74%	–0.39%
Denmark (krone)	5.53%	–0.41%	5.12%	–0.72%	0.69%	–0.03%
New Zealand (dollar)	4.55%	–0.70%	3.85%	–1.92%	1.16%	–0.76%
Singapore (dollar)	4.83%	0.04%	4.87%	–0.19%	–0.07%	–0.26%
South Africa (rand)	6.71%	–1.99%	4.72%	–3.51%	3.32%	–0.19%
Thailand (baht)	5.31%	–0.31%	5.00%	–0.63%	0.52%	–0.11%

ICAPM and Cost of Capital

The traditional expression for asset *i*'s cost of capital in our ICAPM is the factor risk premium form shown in equation (2.1):

International CAPM (ICAPM)

Traditional Factor Risk Premium Form

$$k_i^H = r_f^H + \beta_i'^H \left[GRP^H \right] + \gamma_i'^H \left[XRP^H \right] \tag{2.1}$$

In equation (2.1), $\beta_i'^H$ and $\gamma_i'^H$ are asset i's risk coefficients, where the prime (') notation indicates that the risk coefficients are the <u>partial</u> coefficients in a <u>multivariate regression</u> of asset i's return on two independent variables: (1) the global market index return, and (2) the foreign currency index return. (To simplify notation, we do not use a second subscript to denote G or X in the risk factors.) The interpretation of $\beta_i'^H$ and $\gamma_i'^H$ is like their standard beta and FX exposure counterparts, β_i^H and γ_i^H, except that $\beta_i'^H$ and $\gamma_i'^H$ include adjustments for the systematic connection between the global market index and the foreign currency index.[3]

We now show by example that the ICAPM risk–return expression in equation (2.1) reconciles with a U.S. market index risk premium of 5.65%, using the 1999 to 2016 data and $\Theta = 2.50$. Letting asset i be the U.S. local market index, the <u>partial</u> risk coefficient estimates using Excel regression and 1999 to 2016 data are: $\beta_U'^\$ = 1.005$ and $\gamma_U'^\$ = -0.353$, where the U subscript denotes the U.S. equity index is asset i. Equation (2.1) says that the U.S. market risk premium should be $1.005[0.0592] - 0.353[0.0081] = 0.0565$, or 5.65%.

The assumption of $\Theta = 2.50$ for the chapter's examples is for the deliberate purpose of "anchoring" the ICAPM illustrations to the 5.65% U.S. market risk premium estimate justified in the previous chapter.[4] Of course, the choice of 5.65% for the U.S. market risk premium is arbitrary, but it is important to see how the various risk premium estimates, in the different currencies, are all linked by a specified global market price of risk.

Let $GRP^{A\$} = 3.29\%$ and $XRP^{A\$} = -1.23\%$, per Exhibit 2.2. The Australian equity index's <u>partial</u> risk coefficient estimates (using Excel regression and 1999 to 2016 data) are: $\beta_i'^{A\$} = 0.689$ and $\gamma_i'^{A\$} = -0.702$. Assuming $r_f^{A\$} = 3.50\%$, find the cost of equity and local market risk premium for the Australian equity index in Australian dollars using the traditional ICAPM risk–return expression in equation (2.1).

Answer: Equation (2.1) says that the Australian equity index's cost of equity is $0.035 + 0.689[0.0329] - 0.702[-0.0123] = 0.0663$, or 6.63%. The Australian local equity market risk premium is $6.63\% - 3.50\% = 3.13\%$.

Equation (2.2) shows an alternative ICAPM risk–return relation that is equivalent to the traditional expression in equation (2.1), but uses <u>standard risk coefficients</u> rather than the partial ones:[5]

International CAPM (ICAPM)

Standard Risk Coefficient Form

$$k_i^H = r_f^H + \beta_i^H \left[GRP_1^H \right] + \gamma_i^H \left[XRP_1^H \right] \qquad (2.2)$$

As before, k_i^H is asset i's required return in currency H, and r_f^H is the currency-H risk-free rate. Instead of the more complex partial risk coefficients, the risk coefficients in equation (2.2) have the standard interpretation: β_i^H is asset i's (global) beta for the currency-H perspective, and γ_i^H is asset i's FX exposure to the foreign currency index for the currency-H perspective. The factor risk premiums in equation (2.2) are also not those in equation (2.1), but instead are GRP_1^H and XRP_1^H, the first components of GRP^H and XRP^H, respectively.

To illustrate the ICAPM risk–return expression in equation (2.2), again let asset i be the U.S. market index, and replace the i subscript with U. The U.S. market index's global beta estimate, $\beta_U^\$$, is 0.939, and the U.S. market index's estimated FX exposure to the foreign currency index, $\gamma_U^\$$, is 0.887 (per Exhibit 2.3). Using the $GRP_1^\$$ and $XRP_1^\$$ estimates per Exhibit 2.2, equation (2.2) gives the U.S. market risk premium estimate: $k_U^\$ - r_f^\$ = 0.939[0.0635] + 0.887[-0.0035] = 0.0565$, or 5.65%, as found using equation (2.1).

Assume that in Australian dollars the Australian equity market index has the standard risk coefficient estimates of $\beta_i^{A\$} = 0.603$ and $\gamma_i^{A\$} = -0.595$, per Exhibit 2.3. Per Exhibit 2.2, assume $GRP_1^{A\$} = 3.54\%$ and $XRP_1^{A\$} = -1.65\%$. Assume $r_f^{A\$} = 3.50\%$. Find the cost of equity for the Australian equity market index and the Australian equity market risk premium, in Australian dollars, using the ICAPM risk–return expression in equation (2.2).

Answers: The cost of equity, $k_i^{A\$}$, is equal to $0.035 + 0.603[0.0354] - 0.595[-0.0165] = 0.0662$, or 6.62%. The Australian equity market risk premium is $k_i^{A\$} - r_f^{A\$} = 0.0662 - 0.035 = 0.0312$, or 3.12%. The answers reconcile with the previous boxed example answers, considering rounding of inputs.

The ICAPM traditional factor risk premium form in equation (2.1) is more well-known than the standard risk coefficient form in equation (2.2). However, the benefit of using equation (2.2) is the specification in terms of standard beta and FX exposure inputs, as opposed to the partial beta and FX exposure measures in equation (2.1). This feature makes equation (2.2) advantageous for analyses in subsequent chapters.

ICAPM Versus GCAPM

The ICAPM is a theoretically stronger international risk–return model than the GCAPM, but as you have seen, the ICAPM is more complex than the GCAPM. So, a natural question is how much difference does it make in required return estimates if one uses the simpler GCAPM instead of the more complex, but theoretically superior ICAPM.

Using the "correct" (ICAPM) global risk premium estimate in US dollars (5.92%), and the local U.S. market index's global beta estimate, 0.939, the GCAPM estimate for the U.S. local market risk premium is $0.939[0.0592] = 0.0556$, or 5.56%, which is reasonably close to the "correct" (ICAPM) estimate of 5.65%. For the Australian dollar perspective, on the other hand, if one uses the "correct" (ICAPM) global risk premium estimate in Australian dollars (3.29%), and the Australian local market index's global beta estimate, 0.603, the GCAPM estimate for the Australian local equity market risk premium is $0.603[0.0329] = 0.0198$, or 1.98%, which is 114 basis points below the "correct" (ICAPM) estimate, 3.12%, found in the last boxed example.

For 31 local equity market indexes, including 10 individual Eurozone countries and the Eurozone in aggregate (using the EMU Index), Exhibit 2.3 compares the ICAPM and GCAPM equity market risk premium estimates in local currency for the 1999 to 2016 data. Country Y's ICAPM market risk premium estimate is based on equation (2.2), using the estimates for the country index's global beta, β_Y^C, and FX exposure to the foreign currency index, γ_Y^C, as shown in Exhibit 2.3. The other inputs used in equation (2.2) are shown in Exhibit 2.1. Country Y's GCAPM market risk premium estimate is equal to the country index's global beta estimate times the local currency's "correct" (ICAPM) global market risk premium estimate, GRP^C, per Exhibit 2.2.

Exhibit 2.3 ICAPM vs. GCAPM Local Market Risk Premium Estimates

Global Market Price of Risk = 2.50				
Statistical Parameter Estimation Period: 1999–2016				
	β_Y^C	γ_Y^C	ICAPM	GCAPM
United States (dollar)	0.939	0.887	5.65%	5.56%
Eurozone (euro)	1.062	−0.156	6.03%	5.44%
Japan (yen)	0.723	0.888	5.34%	5.23%
China (yuan)	1.187	2.194	6.87%	6.92%
Britain (pound)	0.830	0.112	4.56%	4.31%
Canada (dollar)	0.848	−0.826	3.96%	3.23%
Australia (dollar)	0.603	−0.595	3.12%	1.98%
Taiwan (dollar)	0.924	−2.132	5.10%	4.55%
Switzerland (franc)	0.668	0.398	4.25%	3.99%
India (rupee)	0.800	−1.529	4.77%	3.70%
Korea (won)	0.945	−0.889	5.16%	3.60%
Brazil (real)	0.255	−0.186	5.22%	1.86%
Mexico (peso)	0.964	−0.612	4.59%	3.66%
Sweden (krona)	1.270	−0.527	6.18%	5.31%
Hong Kong (dollar)	1.047	2.261	6.15%	6.19%
Norway (krone)	0.960	−0.884	5.80%	4.37%
Denmark (krone)	0.923	0.177	4.98%	4.73%
New Zealand (dollar)	0.389	−0.346	2.43%	1.50%
Singapore (dollar)	1.021	−2.111	5.34%	4.98%
South Africa (rand)	0.526	−0.163	4.10%	2.48%
Thailand (baht)	0.789	−1.509	5.13%	3.94%
Germany (euro)	1.22	−0.08	6.84%	6.26%
France (euro)	1.02	−0.14	5.76%	5.20%
Italy (euro)	0.90	−0.37	5.33%	4.62%
Netherlands (euro)	1.06	0.01	5.86%	5.43%
Belgium (euro)	0.91	−0.18	5.22%	4.67%
Ireland (euro)	0.99	0.15	5.36%	5.08%
Spain (euro)	0.92	−0.42	5.48%	4.71%
Austria (euro)	0.92	−0.66	5.70%	4.71%
Finland (euro)	1.44	0.15	7.84%	7.37%
Portugal (euro)	0.68	−0.39	4.11%	3.47%

Exhibit 2.3 shows that for three countries (in addition to the United States), the GCAPM gives a very close approximation to the "correct" (ICAPM) estimate of the country's local equity market risk premium: Japan, China, and Hong Kong. Other countries for which the difference is under 30 basis points, and therefore where the GCAPM's estimates may be a reasonable approximation to the ICAPM's estimates include Britain, Switzerland, Denmark, and Ireland.

On the other hand, there are many countries where the difference between the GCAPM and "correct" (ICAPM) local market risk premium estimates is more than 60 basis points, and the difference is more than 100 basis points for eight countries: Australia, India, Korea, Brazil, Norway, South Africa, Thailand, and Austria.

Bear in mind that Country Y's local equity market index represents Country Y's "average stock." The difference between the ICAPM and GCAPM cost of equity estimates for individual stocks may be higher than that for the "average stock."

As a case in point, Exhibit 2.3 indicates the difference between the ICAPM and GCAPM risk premium estimates for the local British equity index is 25 basis points, yet the next boxed example problem shows that the difference between Rio Tinto's ICAPM and GCAPM cost of equity estimates in British pounds is 80 basis points.

Assume that in British pounds Rio Tinto's ordinary shares have standard risk coefficient estimates of $\beta_i^£ = 1.27$ and $\gamma_i^£ = -0.42$. Per Exhibit 2.2, assume that $GRP_1^£ = 5.59\%$, $XRP_1^£ = -0.71\%$, and $GRP^£ = 5.20\%$. Assume $r_f^£ = 3.50\%$. (a) Find the cost of equity in British pounds for Rio Tinto using the ICAPM risk–return expression in equation (2.2). (b) Compare the answer in (a) to the GCAPM cost of equity estimate.

Answers: (a) Rio Tinto's cost of equity estimate with the ICAPM expression in equation (2.2) is $k_i^£ = 0.035 + 1.27[0.0559] - 0.42[-0.0071] = 0.109$, or 10.9%. (b) The GCAPM estimate is $0.035 + 1.27[0.0520] = 0.101$, or 10.1%, which is 80 basis points lower than the ICAPM estimate.

An empirical study of ICAPM and GCAPM cost of equity estimates for individual U.S. stocks for the 1985 to 2012 period found an average cost of equity difference of only 32 basis points. This average difference is relatively small, especially considering the sample included many small companies. Thus, the study's results indicate that the simpler GCAPM may provide an acceptable approximation to the more complex ICAPM for US dollar cost of equity estimates of U.S. companies.[6] Although there is no empirical research yet that compares ICAPM and GCAPM cost of equity estimates for individual stocks of other countries and currencies, the results in Exhibit 2.3 suggest that GCAPM cost of equity estimates are not good approximations of ICAPM estimates, on average, for many countries.

An Asset's Required Return in Different Currencies

Just as an asset's rate of return is different from the perspective of different currencies, per equation (1.1a), an asset's *required* rate of return, or cost of capital, is different from the perspective of different currencies. So, you must be careful to specify which currency you are using to express a cost of capital. Different cost of equity numbers in different currencies are separate ways to express the same cost of equity. This idea is the same as saying that a firm's equity has only one value, but it is a different number when expressed in different currencies. That is, you can express a firm's equity value either as $100 or Sf 160 given a spot FX rate of 1.60 Sf/$.

Despite being different numbers, a given asset's cost of capital estimates in different currencies must be mutually consistent with each other. To better understand what this means, say an angel were to post online the true expected future cash flow per share for BHP Billiton, and the angel provides this information from both the Australian dollar and US dollar perspectives. BHP Billiton's cost of equity in Australian dollars must be consistent with the cost of equity in US dollars in the following way: If the $/A$ FX rate is correctly valued and expected to be correctly valued in the future, the present (discounted) value of the expected cash flows in the Australian dollar perspective is equivalent at today's spot FX rate to the present (discounted) value of the expected cash flows in the US dollar perspective.

The theory that underlies the ICAPM implicitly assures us that the estimates of a given asset's cost of capital in different currencies are consistent with each other. However, the GCAPM does <u>not</u> give consistent cross-currency cost of capital estimates; the reason is technical and beyond the scope here to cover in detail.[7]

Summary Action Points

- The international CAPM (ICAPM) is theoretically superior to the GCAPM as a risk–return model.
- The GCAPM may provide cost of equity estimates that are reasonable approximations to ICAPM estimates from some currency perspectives, including the US dollar.
- The GCAPM may <u>not</u> provide cost of equity estimates that are reasonable approximations to ICAPM estimates from many non-US dollar perspectives.

Glossary

FX exposure: Sensitivity to changes in FX rates or an index of FX rates, like a beta but with the FX rate(s) replacing the market index.

Partial Risk Coefficients: Risk coefficients (beta and gamma) that are estimated through multiple regression and thus take into consideration the statistical connection of the risk factors.

Standard Risk Coefficients: Risk coefficients (beta and gamma) that are estimated through univariate regression and thus do not take into consideration the statistical connection of the risk factors.

International CAPM (ICAPM): A risk-return model in internationally integrated financial markets in which the global market index replaces the traditional CAPM market index and which has one or more foreign exchange FX risk factors.

Problems

1. Per Exhibit 2.1 for the Swedish krona perspective, $w_{Sk} = 0.008$, $\sigma_G^{Sk} = 0.133$, $\sigma_X^{Sk} = 0.085$, the global market index's estimated FX exposure

to the foreign currency index $\left(\gamma_G^{Sk}\right)$ is 0.22, and the foreign currency index's estimated global beta $\left(\beta_X^{Sk}\right)$ is 0.09. Verify (approximately) the GRP^{Sk} and XRP^{Sk} estimates in Exhibit 2.2 for $\Theta = 2.50$.

2. Assume that in Swedish krona the Sweden equity market index has the <u>standard</u> risk coefficient estimates: $\beta_i^{Sk} = 1.27$ and $\gamma_i^{Sk} = -0.527$, per Exhibit 2.3. Per Exhibit 2.2, let $GRP_1^{Sk} = 4.42\%$ and $XRP_1^{Sk} = -1.07\%$. Use the ICAPM in equation (2.2). (a) Find the market risk premium for the Sweden equity index in Swedish kronor. (b) Assuming $r_f^{Sk} = 2.50\%$, find the cost of equity for the Sweden equity index in Swedish kronor.

3. Let $GRP^{Sk} = 4.18\%$ and $XRP^{Sk} = -0.67\%$, per Exhibit 2.2. Using Excel regression and 1999 to 2016 data, the Sweden equity market index's <u>partial</u> risk coefficient estimates are: $\beta_i'^{Sk} = 1.35$ and $\gamma_i'^{Sk} = -0.82$. Use the ICAPM in equation (2.1). (a) Find the market risk premium for the Sweden equity index in Swedish kronor. (b) Assuming $r_f^{Sk} = 2.50\%$, find the cost of equity for the Sweden equity index in Swedish kronor.

4. Verify the GCAPM estimate of the Sweden equity market risk premium of 5.31%, per Exhibit 2.3.

5. Per Exhibit 2.1 for the Japanese yen perspective, $w_\yen = 0.13$, $\sigma_G^\yen = 0.188$, $\sigma_X^\yen = 0.095$, the global market index's estimated FX exposure to the foreign currency index $\left(\gamma_G^\yen\right)$ is 1.36, and the foreign currency index's estimated global beta $\left(\beta_X^\yen\right)$ is 0.35. Verify (approximately) the $GRP^\yen$ and $XRP^\yen$ estimates in Exhibit 2.2 for $\Theta = 2.50$.

6. Let $GRP^\yen = 7.24\%$ and $XRP^\yen = 1.91\%$, per Exhibit 2.2. Using Excel regression and 1999 to 2016 data, the Japan equity index's <u>partial</u> risk coefficient estimates are: $\beta_i'^\yen = 0.784$ and $\gamma_i'^\yen = -0.182$. Use the ICAPM in equation (2.1). (a) Find the market risk premium for the Japanese equity index in Japanese yen. (b) Assuming $r_f^\yen = 1\%$, find the cost of equity for the Japan equity index in Japanese yen.

7. Assume that in Japanese yen the Japan equity market index has the <u>standard</u> risk coefficient estimates of $\beta_i^\yen = 0.723$ and $\gamma_i^\yen = 0.888$, per Exhibit 2.3. Per Exhibit 2.2, assume $GRP_1^\yen = 8.84\%$ and $XRP_1^\yen = -1.18\%$. Use the ICAPM in equation (2.2). (a) Find the market risk premium for the Japanese equity index in Japanese yen. (b) Assuming $r_f^\yen = 1\%$, find the cost of equity for the Japan equity index in Japanese yen.

8. Verify the GCAPM estimate of the Japan equity market risk premium of 5.23%, per Exhibit 2.3.

Answers to Problems

1. $GRP_1^{Sk} = 2.50(0.133)^2 = 0.0442$, and $GRP_2^{Sk} = (1 - 2.50)(1 - 0.008)$ $(0.22)(0.085)^2 = -0.0024$. Therefore, $GRP^{Sk} = 0.0442 - 0.0024 = 0.0418$, or 4.18%. $XRP_1^{Sk} = (1 - 2.50)(1 - 0.008)(0.085)^2 = -0.0107$, and $XRP_2^{Sk} = 2.50(0.09)(0.133)^2 = 0.0040$. Thus, $XRP^{Sk} = -0.0107 + 0.0040 = -0.0067$, or −0.67%.

2. (a) Per equation (2.2), the Sweden equity index's market risk premium in Swedish kronor is $1.27[0.0442] - 0.527[-0.0107] = 0.0618$, or 6.18%. (b) The cost of equity in kronor for the Sweden equity index is 2.50% + 6.18% = 8.68%.

3. (a) Per equation (2.1), the Sweden equity index's market risk premium in Swedish kronor is $1.35[0.0418] - 0.82[-0.0067] = 0.0619$, or 6.19%. (b) The cost of equity in kronor for the Sweden equity index is 2.50% + 6.19% = 8.69%, which is slightly different from the previous answer due to rounding.

4. $1.27[0.0418] = 0.0531$, or 5.31%, which is 87 basis points lower than the ICAPM estimate of 6.18%.

5. $GRP_1^{¥} = 2.50(0.188)^2 = 0.0884$, and $GRP_2^{¥} = (1 - 2.50)(1 - 0.13)$ $(1.36)(0.095)^2 = -0.016$. $GRP^{¥} = 0.0884 - 0.016 = 0.0724$, or 7.24%. $XRP_1^{¥} = (1 - 2.50)(1 - 0.13)(0.0.095)^2 = -0.0118$, and $XRP_2^{¥} = 2.50(0.35)(0.188)^2 = 0.0309$. Thus, $XRP^{¥} = -0.0118 + 0.0309 = 0.0191$, or 1.91%.

6. (a) Per equation (2.1), the Japan equity index's market risk premium in Japanese yen is $0.785[0.0724] - 0.182[0.0191] = 0.0534$, or 5.34%. (b) The cost of equity in yen for the Japan equity index is 1% + 5.34% = 6.34%.

7. (a) Per equation (2.2), the Japan equity index's market risk premium in Japanese yen is $0.723[0.0884] + 0.888[-0.0118] = 0.0534$, or 5.34%, which reconciles with problem 6, using equation (2.1). (b) The cost of equity in yen for the Japan equity index is 1% + 5.34% = 6.34%.

8. $0.723[0.0724] = 0.0523$, or 5.23%, which is 11 basis points lower than the ICAPM estimate of 5.34%.

Discussion Questions

1. Discuss the pros and cons of using the ICAPM as a risk–return model.

2. The GCAPM is an acceptable risk–return model from some currency perspectives but not others. Discuss.

CHAPTER 3

Hurdle Rates for Overseas Operations

Many companies consist of different business operations in the form of divisions and subsidiaries. For a company's individual business operations, the cost of capital is a concept that is central to valuation, investment (and divestment) decisions, measures of economic profit, and performance appraisal. Finance theory says that an operation has a cost of capital based on that specific operation's risk.

An operation's cost of capital is typically the basis of the operation's *hurdle rate*. In principle, if the operation's actual rate of return is not expected to be at least the operation's hurdle rate, the operation is not adding shareholder value to the parent company. Alternatively, if the present value of the operation's expected cash flows, discounted using the hurdle rate, is not higher than the operation's invested capital, the operation is not adding shareholder value.

In global finance, the idea of operation-specific hurdle rates based on risk means that operations in different countries should have different hurdle rates. As a case in point, Dan Cohrs, the vice president and treasurer at the telecommunications company GTE Corporation in 1996, said that GTE did in fact set different hurdle rates for the company's operations and projects in different countries.[1] This approach does not mean that one hurdle rate in US dollars should simply be converted into different but equivalent rates in different currencies, but that the operations in different countries have different hurdle rates from the perspective of the parent company's home currency, based on the operations' different risks.

Although no single best practice has been established to address the complicated issue of operation-specific hurdle rates, the aim of this chapter is to show some basics of how a firm might estimate an overseas operation's hurdle rate, from the home currency's perspective. For an operation in a developed country, the cost of capital and the hurdle are the same thing. For an operation in an emerging market country, the operation's hurdle rate should reflect a consideration for *political risk* in addition to the cost of capital.

Operation-Specific Risk and Cost of Capital

We should think of an operation's cost of capital as the expected rate of return that would be required on investing in the operation by the aggregate financial market, as compensation for risk, if the operation were an independently traded, all-equity company with no off-balance sheet risk management positions. Therefore, an individual operation's cost of capital differs from the parent firm's overall cost of capital if the operation's risk is different from the parent firm's overall risk. If an operation has higher risk than the parent's overall risk, the operation's hurdle rate should be higher than the parent's overall cost of capital. If the parent's overall cost of capital were used as basis of the operation's hurdle rate, the manager may make investments that do not offer enough expected reward to compensate for the risk. If an operation has lower risk than the parent's overall risk, the operation's hurdle rate should be lower than the parent's overall cost of capital. A manager who does not recognize this may miss out on value-adding investment opportunities by setting the operation's hurdle rate too high.[2]

One reason an overseas operation's risk is likely to differ from the parent company's overall risk is that the operation and the rest of the company are likely to have different systematic relationships with the global economy. For example, the sales volume or the operating costs of a subsidiary in Switzerland may have a different systematic relationship with the global economy than does the rest of the parent company.

Explicitly or implicitly, market investors require a rate of return on their investments based on risk. As we saw in Chapter 1, the market's required rate of return on a company's shares is the company's *cost of equity*. A firm's cost of equity is one component of its *weighted average cost of capital*, or *WACC*, which you probably recall from prior finance courses. A firm's *WACC* is relatively straightforward to calculate, and *WACCs* are used for many purposes in corporate finance; thus, many companies compute a *WACC*. Finance theory tells us that a firm's *WACC* reflects the risk of the enterprise, including the impact of any debt tax shield values and financial risk management positions.

The *WACC* is a useful cost of capital concept for an overall company, but impractical for individual operations, which do not have their own capital structure and market data to compute a *WACC*. Moreover, we do not know how to adjust a parent's overall *WACC* to find a cost of capital for an operation whose risk level varies from the overall risk level of the parent. Because of the problems of applying the *WACC* idea to individual operations, we instead apply risk–return theory directly to individual operations.[3]

WACC Versus Direct Cost of Capital

A cost of capital found directly using a risk–return model is technically slightly different from a *WACC*. In theory, a direct cost of capital discounts the expected operating cash flow stream to the intrinsic business value ("unlevered value"), whereas a *WACC* discounts the expected operating cash flow stream to the intrinsic enterprise value (or "levered value"). The reason is that the standard *WACC* calculation uses the after-tax cost of debt. So, using the *WACC* to capitalize an expected operating cash flow stream includes the value of the debt tax shield and thus results in an estimate of the firm's intrinsic enterprise value.

Business Betas and Proxy Approach

The direct approach to the cost of capital for individual operations uses the idea of *business beta*, which is the beta the operation would have in the absence of debt, cash and marketable securities, and off-balance sheet financial risk management strategies. Sometimes a business beta is called an *all-equity beta*. By beta, we will always mean global beta without saying "global" each time. With a division's estimated business beta, we will use a GCAPM or ICAPM risk–return model to help estimate an operation's cost of capital.

Estimating the business beta for an individual operation has its own problems, because a business beta is not directly observable, and there are typically no historical return data to use in statistical estimation for individual operations. So, we need to be somewhat creative when estimating operation-specific business betas. We rely on the *proxy firm* approach to estimating the business beta for an overseas division. The method is not perfect, but is relatively simple and should be helpful.

In the proxy firm approach, you identify a firm (or firms) with traded equity and in a similar business as the operation. Sometimes, the parent firm itself is a suitable proxy firm if the firm is focused in a relatively homogeneous industry. For example, if a U.S. multinational telecommunications company wants to find the cost of capital for one of its overseas telecommunications subsidiaries, the parent is a reasonable choice for a proxy firm. In more diversified situations, a better proxy choice would be a different firm with a relatively homogenous business like the operation's.

The idea is to estimate the business beta of the proxy firm, but this task is not as straightforward as estimating an equity beta with historical data, because there are typically no market observations of the firm's business value. Instead, we must *unlever* the proxy firm's equity beta estimate to get an estimate of the proxy firm's business beta. To properly unlever an equity beta, we in principle should consider the systematic risk of the firm's net debt and off-balance sheet financial risk management positions. For practical purposes, however, we ignore these items, and in many cases, we will still get a reasonable business beta estimate using the beta unlevering formula in equation (3.1):

Beta Unlevering Formula

$$\beta_B^C = \beta_S^C \left[1 - ND^C / V_B^C \right] \qquad (3.1)$$

In equation (3.1), β_B^C is the business beta, β_S^C is the equity beta, ND^C is net debt, and V_B^C is the business value. All variables are measured from the perspective of currency C. Typically, you can use enterprise value for V_B^C, ignoring that there may be some tax shield value embedded in the enterprise value.[4]

As a (hypothetical) example, assume that a U.S. parent with diversified global operations thinks that the U.S. firm Anderson-Wheeler Company is a reasonable proxy firm for one of its overseas operations. Anderson-Wheeler's estimated equity beta (in US dollars) is 1.20, equity market cap is $60 million, net debt is $20 million ($30 million of debt and $10 million of cash and marketable securities.) Moreover, assume that Anderson-Wheeler has no off-balance sheet risk management positions with systematic risk, and its net debt is denominated entirely in US dollars and has no systematic risk. Ignoring debt tax shield value, the estimated business value is the enterprise value, $60 million + 20 million = $80 million. The ratio of net debt to business value, $ND^\$/V_B^\$$, is $20 million/$80 million = 0.25. Using equation (3.1), Anderson-Wheeler's estimated business beta (in US dollars) is $1.20[1 - 0.25] = 0.90$.

Grand Valley Resources Co. is a U.S. firm with an equity beta esti-mate in US dollars of 0.80, an equity market cap of $100 million, and net debt of $25 million ($35 million of debt and $10 million of cash). Grand Valley has no off-balance sheet financial risk manage-ment positions with systematic risk, the debt tax shield value is zero, and all net debt is denominated in US dollars and has no systematic risk. Find Grand Valley's estimated business beta in US dollars.

Answer: Grand Valley's business value is the enterprise value, $125 million. The ratio of net debt to business value is $25 million/$125 million = 0.20. Using equation (3.1), the business beta estimate in US dollars is 0.80[1 - 0.20] = 0.64.

Regardless of the overseas operation's country, the GCAPM may serve as the risk–return model if the parent company is based in a currency area where the GCAPM gives an acceptable cost of capital approximation to the ICAPM, as in the United States. For parent companies in countries where the GCAPM does not give an acceptable approximation to the ICAPM, we use the ICAPM approach of Chapter 2, which for equation (2.2) requires two risk parameters: (1) beta; and (2) FX exposure to a foreign currency index. If you have estimated a proxy firm's equity beta and FX equity exposure to the foreign currency index, you will need to unlever both risk parameters. To unlever an FX equity exposure estimate, γ_S^C, you can use an equation is analogous to equation (3.1), but specified in terms of FX business and equity exposures to a foreign currency index:

$$\gamma_B^C = \gamma_S^C \left[1 - ND^C/V_B^C\right].$$

Home Country Proxy Firm

If a parent company identifies a suitable proxy firm (or firms) in the home country, one approach to estimating an overseas operation's business beta is the *Lessard country beta method*. This method starts with the proxy's business beta estimate, β_{BP}^{H}, where H denotes the parent firm's home currency. The next step is to estimate the *country beta* of the overseas country's equity market index. Country Y's country beta from the perspective of currency H, β_{Y}^{H}, is the systematic risk of an index fund of country Y's stocks from the currency-H perspective, and is the beta of regressing country Y's equity index returns against the global market index returns, expressing both index returns in currency H.

Exhibit 3.1 shows some country beta estimates from both the US dollar and euro perspectives (based on the 1999 to 2016 data described in Chapter 2). Exhibit 3.1 also shows the analogous estimates for country FX exposure to the foreign currency index, γ_{Y}^{H}, which from the euro perspective are useful in the following examples where we apply the ICAPM. Even though the examples use the GCAPM when the home currency is the US dollar, the country FX exposure estimates from the US dollar perspective are shown anyway. (Note that the country index risk coefficients in Exhibit 2.3 are from the local currency perspective, whereas those in Exhibit 3.1 are in US dollars or euros.)[5]

The last step is to get the home-currency business beta estimate for overseas operation i, β_{Bi}^{H}, by multiplying the home country proxy firm's business beta times the ratio of the overseas country beta to the home country beta, β_{H}^{H}, as shown in equation (3.2). Since this method is adapted from the one pioneered by MIT finance professor Donald Lessard, we call equation (3.2) the *Lessard country beta method*.[6]

Country Beta Method (Lessard)

$$\beta_{Bi}^{H} = \beta_{BP}^{H} \times \left[\beta_{Y}^{H} / \beta_{H}^{H} \right] \tag{3.2}$$

For example, say a U.S. multinational wants to estimate the cost of capital (in US dollars) for a subsidiary in Sweden. A home country proxy firm has a business beta estimate of 0.50. Assume that in US dollars, the Sweden country beta is 1.45 and the U.S. country beta is 0.94, as in Exhibit 3.1.

Exhibit 3.1 Country Beta and FX Exposure Estimates

In US Dollars and Euros				
Estimation Period: 1999–2015				
	$\beta_Y^{\$}$	$\gamma_Y^{\$}$	$\beta_Y^{\euro}$	$\gamma_Y^{\euro}$
United States (dollar)	0.94	0.89	1.02	0.67
Eurozone (euro)	1.26	1.90	1.06	−0.16
Japan (yen)	0.74	1.06	0.81	0.78
China (yuan)	1.19	1.65	1.16	0.25
Britain (pound)	0.96	1.46	0.88	0.29
Canada (dollar)	1.12	1.56	1.09	0.38
Australia (dollar)	1.16	1.95	0.99	0.01
Taiwan (dollar)	1.08	1.12	1.13	0.57
Switzerland (franc)	0.82	1.54	0.67	0.17
India (rupee)	1.18	1.68	1.12	0.28
Korea (won)	1.43	1.76	1.45	0.47
Brazil (real)	1.68	2.50	1.51	−0.06
Mexico (peso)	1.21	1.32	1.27	0.52
Sweden (krona)	1.44	1.73	1.35	0.07
Hong Kong (dollar)	1.05	1.40	1.06	0.52
Norway (krone)	1.43	2.31	1.20	−0.21
Denmark Krone)	1.04	1.67	0.92	0.13
New Zealand (dollar)	0.95	1.69	0.82	0.13
Singapore (dollar)	1.14	1.58	1.13	0.43
South Africa (rand)	1.20	2.03	1.06	0.11
Thailand (baht)	1.21	1.95	1.16	0.37
Germany (euro)	1.38	1.85	1.22	−0.08
France (euro)	1.21	1.85	1.02	−0.14
Italy (euro)	1.19	2.07	0.90	−0.37
Netherlands (euro)	1.20	1.69	1.06	0.01
Belgium (euro)	1.13	1.94	0.91	−0.18
Ireland (euro)	1.07	1.43	0.99	0.15
Spain (euro)	1.23	2.24	0.92	−0.42
Austria (euro)	1.30	2.62	0.92	−0.66
Finland (euro)	1.50	1.69	1.44	0.15
Portugal (euro)	1.00	2.10	0.68	−0.39

Using equation (3.2), the business beta estimate in US dollars for the Swedish subsidiary is 0.50[1.45/0.94] = 0.77. Since Sweden's country beta is higher than the home country (U.S.) beta, it makes sense that the Swedish subsidiary's business beta estimate is higher than the home country (U.S.) proxy's business beta estimate. This method is ad hoc, but is practical.

Assume that a U.S. multinational company wants to estimate a business beta for its Swiss subsidiary from the home currency (US dollar) perspective. The business beta estimate of a typical U.S. firm in the same industry as the subsidiary is 0.90. Assume that the country beta estimate in US dollars of the Swiss equity market index is 0.82, and the U.S. country beta is 0.94, per Exhibit 3.1. Use the Lessard country beta method to find the Swiss subsidiary's business beta estimate?

Answer: In US dollars, the business beta estimate for the Swiss subsidiary is 0.90[0.82/0.94] = 0.79.

For parent companies in countries where it's better to use the ICAPM of Chapter 2, we should adjust a home country proxy firm's FX business exposure to the foreign currency index, γ_{BP}^H, to get operation i's FX business exposure estimate from the home currency perspective, γ_{Bi}^H. But a multiplicative approach like equation (3.2) does not work because FX exposures can be either positive or negative. So, the adjustment is to simply add the difference between the FX exposure estimates for the overseas and home country equity market indexes, $\gamma_Y^H - \gamma_H^H$, as shown in equation (3.3):

Country FX Exposure Method

$$\gamma_{Bi}^H = \gamma_{BP}^H + \left[\gamma_Y^H - \gamma_H^H\right] \tag{3.3}$$

For example, say an Italian parent firm uses the ICAPM in equation (2.2) to estimate the cost of capital for a Swedish operation in the parent's home currency, euros. After unlevering the equity beta and FX equity exposure estimates, the home country proxy firm's estimated business beta, $\beta_{BP}^{\unicode{8364}}$, is 1.20, and FX business exposure to the foreign currency index, $\gamma_{BP}^{\unicode{8364}}$, is 0.60. From the euro perspective (per Exhibit 3.1), Sweden's country beta is 1.35 and country FX exposure is 0.07, and Italy's country beta is 0.90

and country FX exposure is −0.37. Using equation (3.2), the Swedish operation's business beta estimate (in euros), $\beta_{Bi}^{\text{€}}$, is $1.20[1.35/0.90] = 1.80$; using equation (3.3), the operation's FX business exposure estimate from the euro perspective, $\gamma_{Bi}^{\text{€}}$, is $0.60 + [0.07 − (−0.37)] = 1.04$.

Once you have an overseas operation's business risk estimate(s) in the home currency, you can use a risk–return equation to calculate the direct home-currency estimate of the overseas operation's cost of capital, k_{Bi}^{H}. For example, let an overseas operation's business beta estimate in US dollars be 0.90. To get a cost of capital in US dollars, we use the GCAPM. If the risk-free rate in US dollars is 3% the global risk premium in US dollars is 6%, the division's $k_{Bi}^{\$}$ estimate is equal to $r_f^{\$} + \beta_{Bi}^{\$}[GRP^{\$}] = 0.03 + 0.90[0.06] = 0.084$, or 8.40%.

The Italian parent above uses the ICAPM in equation (2.2) to estimate the Swedish division's cost of capital in euros. Assume that the risk-free rate in euros is 2.5%, and $GRP_1^{\text{€}} = 5.54\%$ and $XRP_1^{\text{€}} = −0.92\%$, per Exhibit 2.2. Therefore, the Swedish operation's cost of capital in euros is $k_{Bi}^{\text{€}} = 0.025 + 1.80[0.0554] + 1.04[−0.0092] = 0.115$, or 11.5%.

A German multinational company uses the ICAPM to estimate the cost of capital for a Swiss operation in the parent's home currency, euros. The parent has found a suitable home country proxy firm, and after unlevering the proxy's equity beta and FX equity exposure estimates, has estimated that in euros, the proxy's business beta, $\beta_{BP}^{\text{€}}$, is 0.75, and FX business exposure to the foreign currency index, $\gamma_{BP}^{\text{€}}$, is 0.40. From the euro perspective, Switzerland's country beta is 0.67 and country FX exposure is 0.17, and Germany's country beta is 1.22 and country FX exposure is −0.08, per Exhibit 3.1. Use the ICAPM in equation (2.2) to estimate the Swiss operation's cost of capital in euros, assuming: (1) the risk-free rate in euros is 2.5%; and (2) $GRP_1^{\text{€}} = 5.54\%$ and $XRP_1^{\text{€}} = −0.92\%$, per Exhibit 2.2.

Answer: Using equation (3.2), the Swiss operation's business beta estimate (from the euro perspective), $\beta_{Bi}^{\text{€}}$, is $0.75[0.67/1.22] = 0.41$. Using equation (3.3), the Swiss operation's FX business exposure estimate to the currency index from the euro perspective, $\gamma_{Bi}^{\text{€}}$, is $0.40 + [0.17 − (−0.08)] = 0.65$. The Swiss operation's cost of capital estimate, in euros, is equal to $k_{Bi}^{\text{€}} = 0.025 + 0.41[0.0554] + 0.65[−0.0092] = 0.0417$, or 4.17%.

Political Risk and Emerging Market Operations

For operations in many emerging market countries, analysts like to consider *political risk* in addition to the standard systematic economic/financial risk in risk–return models. *Political risk* is a catch-all term used to describe the additional risks posed in terms of illiquidity, civil disruptions, corruption, political intervention, expropriation, imposition of controls on funds repatriation, irresponsible economic management by the country's policymakers, and the like.

There is some disagreement about whether political risk should be an adjustment to an operation's expected cash flows or to the hurdle rate. Since political risk is not a specified systematic risk factor in asset pricing models, some argue that any adjustment for political risk should be made to expected cash flows. But this advice has proven difficult to follow, and so the trend in practice is to include an adjustment for political risk in an emerging market project's hurdle rate.

In principle, a given country's *political risk premium* does not have a currency denomination, and is thus the same number from any currency perspective. Still, political risk premiums are difficult to measure. Many managers and analysts estimate country Y's political risk premium, PRP_y, by the yield on the country's *sovereign credit default swap* (*CDS*), which is an "insurance policy" against the default of a sovereign bond issued by a sovereign country. In general, a CDS is insurance against the default of a bond. As long as the bond does not default, the insurance buyer makes payments to the insurance seller based on the CDS rate. If the bond does default, the insurance buyer delivers the bond to the insurance seller, while the seller pays the buyer the face value of the bond. Figure 3.1 shows the basic idea.

Exhibit 3.2 shows sovereign CDS yields for some emerging market countries for May 31, 2013. The quotes in Exhibit 3.2 are in basis points,

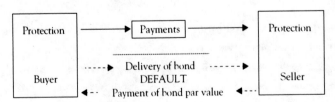

Figure 3.1 Credit default swaps

so the CDS yield for Argentina is 3,144 basis points, or 31.44%. For Chile, the CDS yield is only 76 basis points, or 0.76%. Of course, CDS yields are market prices that change constantly with conditions; those in Exhibit 3.2 are only for illustration purposes.

Many analysts now prefer to base a PRP_Y estimate on a market-driven CDS yield instead of the earlier choice, the *sovereign yield spread*, which is the difference between the yields on sovereign debt issued in US dollars and a long-term U.S. government bond. Technically, however, CDS yields and sovereign yield spreads both measure *sovereign risk*, which is

Exhibit 3.2 Sovereign Credit Default Swap Yields and Political Risk Premium Estimates

Selected Emerging Market Countries			
May 31, 2013			
	CDS_Y	PRP_Y/SRP_Y	PRP_Y
Argentina	3,144	0.31	9.75%
Brazil	146	0.79	1.15%
Bulgaria	120	0.40	0.48%
Chile	76	0.73	0.55%
China	84	1.00	0.84%
Colombia	104	0.87	0.90%
Croatia	310	0.56	1.74%
Egypt	623	0.79	4.92%
Hungary	292	0.32	0.93%
Indonesia	162	0.78	1.26%
Mexico	102	0.70	0.71%
Panama	103	0.82	0.84%
Peru	109	0.86	0.94%
Philippines	97	0.85	0.82%
Poland	76	0.86	0.65%
Russia	155	1.00	1.55%
South Africa	191	0.79	1.51%
Turkey	131	0.79	1.03%
Ukraine	601	0.52	3.13%
Venezuela	840	0.60	5.04%

Source for CDS yields: Bloomberg quotes on Deutsche Bank site (with permission).
Source for Political Risk to Sovereign Risk Ratio Estimates: Adapted from Bekaert et al. (2016).

the risk that the country's government will not service its debt obligations properly. In addition to political risk, sovereign risk entails some macroeconomic and financial risk that is captured in standard measures of systematic risk. So, estimating a political risk premium by either type of sovereign risk premium, SRP_Y, tends to involve some double-counting of systematic risk.

Some researchers have tried to correct for this problem by estimating the percentage of sovereign risk that is represented by political risk, PRP_Y/SRP_Y. Estimates of these percentages are shown for some countries in Exhibit 3.2. For Chile, for example, the CDS yield is 0.76% and political risk is estimated to be 73% of sovereign risk, so the political risk premium estimate would be 0.73(0.76%) = 0.55%. On average, the political risk is 62% of sovereign risk for the 20 countries in Exhibit 3.2. So, if you have a CDS yield estimate for a country, but no estimate of PRP_Y/SRP_Y, consider using $PRP_Y/SRP_Y = 0.62$.[7]

For an emerging market country with political risk, individual assets and operations pose different degrees of *political risk exposure*. The political risk exposure of operation i, denoted Φ_i, is the operation's degree of political risk relative to the overall country's political risk. Some operations may be relatively free of political risk. An example might be a tomato plant in a stable food industry. At the other end of the spectrum are emerging market industries that are highly susceptible to political intervention, like the power and oil industries, or have relatively high potential for corruption.

One simple approach to the problem is to group industries into low, medium, and high political risk exposure categories. The low exposure category includes consumer discretionary and staples; the medium exposure category includes health care, industrials, information technology, materials, telecommunications, and utilities; and the high exposure category includes energy and financials. For operations in the medium exposure category, or if the manager has no opinion about the operation's political risk exposure, the manager should assume that Φ_i is equal to the average political risk exposure for the country, which is 1. For operations with high political risk exposure for the country, Φ_i should be higher than 1, say 1.50. For investments judged to have low political risk exposure, let $\Phi_i = 0.50$.[8]

In some cases, managers may want to make other adjustments in political risk exposure estimates. One example is if a foreign operation has issued its own debt to local investors. This debt may reduce the operation's political risk exposure. Another factor may be the extent to which the operation brings foreign currency into the emerging country. This idea is explored in the box titled "Brazilian Firms Embraer and Embratel." One method in that box is to estimate Φ_i by the ratio of the operation's local revenues to the average local revenues of firms domiciled in the country. For example, Embraer derives only about 3% of its revenues locally, while Embratel derives 95% of its revenues locally. Since the average Brazilian firm generates 77% of its revenues locally, the Φ_i for Embraer would be $0.03/0.77 = 0.04$, and the Φ_i for Embratel would be $0.95/0.77 = 1.23$.[9]

Brazilian Firms Embraer and Embratel

Professor Aswath Damodaran of New York University (NYU) suggests two methods to try to measure a company's Φ_i. He estimated Φ_i for two Brazilian firms: (a) Embraer, an aerospace company that manufactures and sells aircraft to many of the world's leading airlines; and (b) Embratel, the large Brazilian telecommunications company.

The first method is the ratio of the firm's local revenues to the local revenues of the average firm of the country. The more revenues come from outside the country, the lower the Φ_i. Embraer derives only about 3% of its revenues locally, while Embratel derives 95% of its revenues locally. Since the average Brazilian firm generates 77% of its revenues locally, the Φ_i for Embraer would be $0.03/0.77 = 0.04$, and the Φ_i for Embratel would be $0.95/0.77 = 1.23$.

The second method is to estimate Φ_i as the coefficient of a time series of the firm's equity returns (converted to US dollars) against the returns on a Brazilian sovereign bond (converted to US dollars). For Embraer, the estimated Φ_i was 0.27. For Embratel, the Φ_i estimate was 2.00.

In this text, the hurdle rate for emerging market asset i (in the parent's home currency), h_i^H, is the asset's cost of capital, k_i^H, plus the adjustment political risk. The adjustment for political risk is technically not part of the cost of capital but is added to the cost of capital to get the hurdle rate because that's a more practical way of dealing with political risk than adjusting expected cash flows.

You can use either the GCAPM or the ICAPM to capture the cost of capital. Using US dollars as the home currency and the GCAPM as the risk–return model, the cost of capital, $k_i^\$$, is equal to $r_f^\$ + \beta_i^\$ [GRP^\$]$, and the hurdle rate is given in equation (3.4):[10]

Emerging Market Hurdle Rate Model

$$h_i^\$ = r_f^\$ + \beta_i^\$ [GRP^\$] + \Phi_i [PRP_Y] \tag{3.4}$$

For example, assume that a U.S. multinational wants to use the GCAPM and to estimate the hurdle rate in US dollars for its subsidiary in Hungary. Assume: (a) Hungary's political risk premium, PRP_Y, is 0.93%, per Exhibit 3.2; (b) the subsidiary has low political risk exposure, Φ_i, of 0.50; (c) the subsidiary's business beta in US dollars is 0.90; (d) the risk-free rate in US dollars is 3%; and (e) the global risk premium in US dollars is 6%. The Hungarian subsidiary's hurdle rate estimate in US dollars, applying equation (3.4), is $h_{Bi}^\$ = 0.03 + 0.90[0.06] + 0.50[0.0093] = 0.0887$, or 8.87%.

A U.S. multinational power company wants to estimate the hurdle rate in US dollars for power plant project in Ukraine. Management believes the industry has high political risk exposure, and subjectively estimates the operation's Φ_i to be 1.50. The project's estimated business beta (in US dollars) is 0.70, the US dollar risk-free rate is 3%, and the global risk premium in US dollars is 6%. Assume that the GCAPM is the risk–return relationship for systematic risk. Assume that Ukraine's estimated political risk premium is 3.13%, per Exhibit 3.2. Find the project's estimated hurdle rate in US dollars using equation (3.4).

Answer: $h_{Bi}^\$ = 0.03 + 0.70[0.06] + 1.50[0.0313] = 0.119$, or 11.9%.

A New Zealand multinational company wants to estimate the hurdle rate in New Zealand dollars (Z$) for an operation in South Africa. Management believes that the operation's industry is in the low political risk exposure category, and thus estimates the operation's Φ_i to be 0.50. Assume that the ICAPM in equation (2.2) is the risk–return relationship for the cost of capital. Assume: (1) The operation's estimated business beta (in Z$) is 0.80 and estimated FX business exposure to *the foreign currency index (in Z\$) is –0.76; (2) the Z\$ risk-free rate is 4%; (3) $GRP_1^{Z\$} = 4.55\%$ and $XRP_1^{Z\$} = -1.92\%$, per Exhibit 2.2; and (4) South Africa's estimated political risk premium is 1.51%, per Exhibit 3.2. (a) Estimate the operation's cost of capital in Z\$. (b) Estimate the operation's hurdle rate in Z\$.*

Answers: (a) $k_{Bi}^{Z\$} = 0.04 + 0.80[0.0455] - 0.76[-0.0192] = 0.0694$, or 6.94%. (b) $h_{Bi}^{Z\$} = 0.0694 + 0.50[0.0151] = 0.077$, or 7.70%.

Estimating hurdle rates for emerging market operations is clearly a challenging task. The previous suggestions may provide some guidance, but there is plenty of room for subjectivity and judgment. One unanswered question is: How does the level of local investment affect the political risk exposure of an emerging market operation? If a U.S. company produces in the United States and exports the products, does the company's foreign operation have higher or lower political risk exposure than if the foreign operation has a local plant to produce for that market? If the operation has a local plant, there is more to lose in case of political disruption, but the operation might also be seen in a more favorable light by the host government because of the jobs being provided. And what about the political risk for an overseas production operation that ships the products to markets in other countries?

A final note before moving on: Because of sovereign risk, the yield on a country's sovereign bond denominated in local currency is <u>not</u> the currency's risk-free rate. Instead a reasonable estimate of the currency's risk-free rate is the sovereign yield in local currency minus the CDS yield. The reason is that an owner of a country's local-currency sovereign bond who purchases a CDS has engineered a risk-free asset in the local currency. For example, if the yield on Mexican sovereign debt is Mexican pesos is 5.02% and the CDS yield is 1.02%, the Mexican peso risk-free rate is 4%.

Assume that the yield on Indonesian sovereign debt in Indonesian rupiah is 7% and the CDS yield is 1.62%. What is the Indonesian rupiah risk-free rate?

Answer: 7% – 1.62% = 5.38%.

Summary Action Points

- A company's operations in different countries may have different costs of capital, from the perspective of the company's home currency, due to systematic risk differences.
- It is easier to estimate an overseas operation's cost of capital directly with a risk–return model than by a *WACC*.
- A proxy firm is often useful in estimating a foreign operation's systematic risk. If the proxy firm is the parent, or is in the parent's home country, a method using country beta (Lessard), and possibly country FX exposure to a foreign currency index, is useful in estimating the operation's systematic risk(s).
- If an overseas operation is in an emerging market country, its hurdle rate may need to include a premium for political risk in addition to the cost of capital. A CDS yield is useful in estimating a country's political risk premium.

Glossary

Business Beta: (a) The beta an all-equity operation would have if it uses no financial risk management strategies; (b) the beta of the operation's business value.

Cost of Capital for a Business Operation: The rate that discounts the operation's expected future business cash flow steam to the intrinsic business value.

Country Beta: The beta of a country's national equity index versus the global market index.

Credit Default Swap (CDS): A market-traded "insurance policy" against the default of a bond. If the bond does not default, the buyer makes payments based on the CDS yield. If the bond defaults, the buyer delivers the bond to the seller, and the seller pays the buyer the bond's face value.

Hurdle Rate: The rate of return that needs to be expected for an investment to add value. For developed market assets, the hurdle rate is in principle the asset's cost of capital. For emerging market investments, the hurdle rate is the asset's cost of capital plus and adjustment for political risk.

Political Risk: A catch-all term used to describe the additional risks posed by emerging market investments in terms of illiquidity, civil disruptions, corruption, political intervention, expropriation, and the like.

Political Risk Exposure: A foreign asset's political risk relative to the foreign country's overall political risk.

Political Risk Premium: An adjustment for the cost of capital to get the hurdle rate for an emerging market operation that has the average political risk in the emerging market country.

Sovereign Risk: The risk that a country's government will not repay its obligations.

Unlever: To find a business variable (such as business beta) by removing the effect of financial strategies on an equity variable (such as equity beta).

Problems

1. A U.S. firm's equity beta in US dollars is 1.25. The equity market cap is $4 million and net debt is $1 million ($2 million of debt and $1 million of cash). The company has no off-balance sheet risk management positions with systematic risk, and debt and cash are denominated entirely in US dollars. Assume that business value = enterprise value. (a) Find the business beta. (b) The GCAPM is the international risk–return trade-off, viewed in US dollars. Find the cost of capital for business operations, given a US dollar risk-free rate of 3% and a global risk premium of 6% in US dollars.

2. A U.S. firm has an equity beta in US dollars of 1.10. The equity market cap is $6 million, and net debt is $2 million ($3 million of debt and $1 million of cash). The firm has no off-balance sheet risk management positions with systematic risk, and debt and cash are denominated entirely in US dollars. Assume that business value = enterprise value. (a) Find the business beta in US dollars. (b) The GCAPM is the

international risk–return trade-off, viewed in US dollars. The US dollar risk-free rate = 3%. The global risk premium = 6% in US dollars. Find the cost of capital for business operations (in US dollars).

3. The U.S. multinational American Electronics Co. has estimated its overall business beta to be 0.90. In US dollars, the estimated (global) beta is 1.16 for the Australian stock market index, and is 0.94 for the U.S. stock market index. Assume that American Electronics itself is a reasonable U.S. proxy firm for its Australian division. (a) Use the Lessard country beta method to find the Australian division's estimated business beta. (b) The GCAPM is the international risk–return trade-off, viewed in US dollars. The US dollar risk-free rate = 3%. The global risk premium = 6% in US dollars. Find the hurdle rate estimate for the Australian division.

4. A U.S. multinational wants to estimate a hurdle rate for its New Zealand division. The parent's operations are in a homogeneous industry, so the parent's business beta, 0.70, can serve as a U.S. proxy beta. In US dollars, the global beta of the New Zealand stock index is 0.95. The global beta of the U.S. stock index in US dollars is 0.94. Use the Lessard country beta method to find the business beta of the New Zealand division. Ignore political risk. The US dollar risk-free rate is 3% and the global risk premium is 6%. Find the New Zealand division's hurdle rate estimate in US dollars using the GCAPM.

5. A French multinational company uses the ICAPM to estimate the cost of capital for a Canadian operation in the parent's home currency, euros. The home country proxy firm, after unlevering the equity beta and FX equity exposure estimates, has an estimated business beta, β_{BP}^{ϵ}, of 1.05, and a FX business exposure to the foreign currency index, γ_{BP}^{ϵ}, of 0.45. From the euro perspective, Canada's country beta is 1.09 and country FX exposure is 0.38, and France's country beta is 1.02 and country FX exposure is −0.14, per Exhibit 3.1. Use the ICAPM risk–return expression in equation (2.2) to estimate the Canadian division's cost of capital in euros, assuming: (1) the risk-free rate in euros is 2.5%; and (2) $GRP_1^{\epsilon} = 5.54\%$ and $XRP_1^{\epsilon} = -0.92\%$, per Exhibit 2.2.

6. A U.S. multinational wants to estimate the hurdle rate in US dollars for its subsidiary in Bulgaria. Assume that Bulgaria's political risk premium is 0.48%, per Exhibit 3.2. The subsidiary's political risk

exposure is 0.50. The subsidiary's business beta (in US dollars) is 1. The GCAPM is the risk–return trade-off model in US dollars, the US dollar risk-free rate is 3%, and the global risk premium in US dollars is 6%. Find the hurdle rate for the Bulgarian subsidiary in US dollars.

7. A U.S. firm wants to estimate the hurdle rate for its subsidiary in Russia. Assume: (1) Russia has a country beta in US dollars of 1.29; (2) The subsidiary's political risk exposure is 1; (3) The Russian political risk premium is 1%, per Exhibit 3.2; and (4) A U.S. proxy firm has a business beta of 0.90. Further assume: The risk-free rate in US dollars is 3%; the global risk premium in US dollars is 6%; the GCAPM is the risk–return trade-off in US dollars. (a) Find the subsidiary's estimated business beta in US dollars using the Lessard country beta method, assuming the U.S. equity index has a global beta of 0.94. (b) Estimate the project's hurdle rate in US dollars.

8. A U.S. multinational wants to estimate the hurdle rate in US dollars for its operation in Tanzania. Assume that Tanzania's political risk premium is 3.50%. The operation has a business beta in US dollars of 0.75 and is in an industry that has 1.50 times the average political risk for Tanzanian companies. The GCAPM is the risk–return trade-off, viewed in US dollars. The US dollar risk-free rate = 3%. The global risk premium = 6% in US dollars. Find the Tanzanian operation's hurdle rate in US dollars.

9. You are the manager of the Colombian division for a U.S. multinational building materials company. Your division manufactures insulation in the United States and ships it to Colombia, where it is packaged and delivered to the building industry. Assume that the U.S. parent company of your division is a suitable U.S. proxy firm for your division. The parent has a global equity beta in US dollars of 1.20. The parent's equity market cap is $700 million, debt is $400 million, and cash is $100 million. The parent's net debt has no systematic risk, and the parent has no off-balance sheet financial risk management positions with systematic risk. The country beta of the Colombian equity market, in US dollars, is 0.90, and the U.S. equity market's country beta is 0.94. Assume that the political risk premium for Colombia is 3%. Assume that the political risk exposure is equal to 1. The GCAPM is the risk–return trade-off, viewed in US dollars. The US dollar risk-free rate = 3%. The global risk premium = 6%

in US dollars. (a) Estimate the parent's business beta. (b) Use the Lessard country beta method to estimate the division's business beta. (c) Estimate the division's hurdle rate in US dollars.

For 10 to 12: Lincoln Resources Co. is a U.S. multinational company with a business value of $40 billion. Lincoln has actual net debt of $10 billion, all of which is denominated in US dollars. Lincoln has no off-balance sheet risk management positions with systematic risk. Lincoln's estimated global equity beta in US dollars is 1.20. Lincoln's management wants to set the hurdle rate for its operation in Kazakhstan. For the operation's business beta, Lincoln will use the Lessard country beta method with Lincoln's own business beta serving as the U.S. proxy's business beta. The operation is in an industry with a relatively low political risk exposure, so Lincoln assumes the operation's political risk exposure is 0.75. The Kazakhstan currency is the tenge ($\overline{T}$, KZT). Assume: (1) In US dollars, the global beta of the Kazakhstan stock market is 1.70, and the global beta of the U.S. stock index is 0.94. (2) The Kazakhstan political risk premium is 2.50%. (3) The GCAPM is the model of risk and return in US dollars. (4) The US dollar risk-free rate is 3%. (5) The global risk premium is 6% in US dollars.

10. Estimate Lincoln's business beta in US dollars.
11. Estimate the business beta (in US dollars) of the Kazakhstan affiliate using the Lessard country beta method.
12. Estimate the hurdle rate in US dollars for the Kazakhstan operation.

13. Assume that the yield on Colombian sovereign debt in Colombian pesos is 5% and the CDS yield is 1.04%. What is the Colombian peso risk-free rate?

Answers to Problems

1. (a) Business value is $5 million. The ratio of net debt to business value is $1 million/$5 million = 0.20. Using equation (3.1), the business beta is $1.25[1 - 0.20] = 1$. (b) Using the GCAPM, the cost of capital estimate is $0.03 + 1[0.06] = 0.09$, or 9%.
2. (a) Business value is $8 million. The ratio of net debt to business value is $2 million/$8 million = 0.25. Using equation (3.1), the

business beta is $1.10[1 - 0.25] = 0.825$. (b) $k_{Bi}^{\$} = 0.03 + 0.825[0.06]$ $= 0.0795$, or 7.95%.

3. (a) The Australian division's estimated business beta is $0.90[1.16/0.94]$ $= 1.11$. (b) The division's cost of capital estimate in US dollars is $0.03 + 1.11[0.06] = 0.0967$, or 9.67%, which is the hurdle rate, given the practice of ignoring political risk for developed countries.

4. The estimated business beta of the New Zealand division is $0.70[0.95/0.94] = 0.707$. The estimated hurdle rate in US dollars is $0.03 + 0.707[0.06] = 0.072$, or 7.20%.

5. Using equation (3.2), the Canadian operation's business beta estimate (from the euro perspective), $\beta_{Bi}^{\euro}$, is $1.05[1.09/1.02] = 1.12$. Using equation (3.3), the Canadian operation's FX business exposure estimate from the euro perspective, $\gamma_{Bi}^{\euro}$, is $0.45 + [0.38 - (-0.14)] = 0.97$. The Canadian operation's cost of capital estimate, in euros, is equal to $k_{Bi}^{\euro} = 0.025 + 1.12[0.0554] + 0.97[-0.0092] = 0.0781$, or 7.81%.

6. (a) $0.03 + 1[0.06] + 0.50[0.0048] = 0.0924$, or 9.24%

7. (a) $0.90[1.29/0.94] = 1.24$; (b) $0.03 + 1.24[0.06] + 1[0.01] = 0.114$, or 11.4%.

8. $0.03 + 0.75[0.06] + 1.50[0.035] = 0.1275$, or 12.75%.

9. (a) Parent business beta estimate: $1.20[1 - 0.30] = 0.84$.
(b) Division's business beta estimate: $0.84[0.90/0.94] = 0.804$.
(c) $0.03 + 0.804[0.06] + 1[0.03] = 0.108$, or 10.8%.

10. $1.20[1 - 0.25] = 0.90$.

11. $0.90[1.70/0.94] = 1.63$.

12. $0.03 + 1.63[0.06] + 0.75[0.025] = 0.147$, or 14.7%.

13. $5\% - 1.04\% = 3.96\%$.

Discussion Questions

1. Discuss the pros and cons of the chapter's approach for estimating a hurdle rate for an overseas subsidiary or division.
2. Discuss the pros and cons of using a country's sovereign CDS rate as the country's political risk premium.
3. What types of industries do you think would have high political risk exposure? Low political risk exposure?
4. Explain the difference between political risk and sovereign risk.

CHAPTER 4

Converting Hurdle Rates and Expected Cash Flows Across Currencies

The theory of cross-border investments is generally based on the standard concept of discounting a project's expected operating cash flows back to the present using a cost of capital (or hurdle rate) that reflects the risk. An investment's *net present value* (*NPV*) is the present value of the expected cash flows minus the outlay necessary to undertake the investment. If the NPV is positive, the investment should be accepted, because the intrinsic wealth of the firm's existing shareholders would rise. If the NPV is negative, the investment should be rejected, because intrinsic wealth of the firm's existing shareholders would drop.

One issue is whether to consider a foreign investment's entire cash flow or only the portion repatriated. Our answer is immediate: Consider the investment's *entire* cash flow, not just the portion repatriated. The reason is that even the portion reinvested overseas affects the intrinsic wealth of the firm's shareholders, because the reinvestment increases the value that the overseas investment could be sold for, and thus needs to be included in the analysis. So, we consider an overseas investment's entire cash flow, not just the portion repatriated.

Another critical issue is the choice of currency perspective to use for the valuation analysis. In the *home currency approach*, one converts expected foreign currency cash flows into home currency equivalents using forecasted FX rates, and then discounts them using a hurdle rate denominated in the home currency. In the *foreign currency approach*, the analyst uses the expected cash flows denominated in the foreign currency, and discounts them using a hurdle rate denominated in the foreign currency. This chapter addresses how to convert hurdle rates and expected cash flows between currencies.

In the foreign currency approach, managers need to express a foreign operation's cost of capital and hurdle rate in the overseas local currency, given the cost of capital and hurdle rate in the parent company's home currency. For example, a U.S. multinational company may have estimated the hurdle rate for a foreign subsidiary in US dollars, and wants to know the *consistent* hurdle rate in the local foreign currency. Sometimes, the parent will supply a foreign subsidiary's managers with the foreign currency hurdle rate, for making local, decentralized investment decisions.

This chapter shows how to convert a hurdle rate in one currency into an equivalent one expressed in a different currency. As part of this analysis, the chapter covers using the ICAPM to estimate a currency risk premium. Finally, the chapter addresses issues in converting expected cash flows from foreign currency to home currency, for applying the home currency approach to international investment decisions.

Converting a Hurdle Rate to an Overseas Currency

We now address the issue of converting an asset's hurdle rate from one currency to another. To convert a home currency cost of capital estimate for asset i, k_i^H, into an equivalent one in overseas currency C, k_i^C, one can use equation (4.1):

Cost of Capital Conversion

$$1 + k_i^C = \left(1 + k_i^H\right)\left[1 + E^*\left(x^{C/H}\right)\right] - \gamma_{iC}^H\left(\sigma_C^H\right)^2 \qquad (4.1)$$

Equation (4.1) says that you first multiply $(1 + k_i^H)$ times $[1 + E^*(x^{C/H})]$, where $E^*(x^{C/H})$ is the equilibrium expected rate of FX change (or the expected rate of intrinsic FX change) of the home currency versus currency C. The asterisk denotes the idea of equilibrium or intrinsic.

Then, you adjust for the interaction between the asset's return and the FX rate. This interaction adjustment involves γ_{iC}^H, which is asset i's FX exposure to currency C, from the home currency perspective, and which may be estimated by regressing asset i's returns on percentage changes in currency C versus currency H, $x^{H/C}$. The interaction adjustment also involves σ_C^H, the volatility of $x^{H/C}$.

The result is $1 + k_i^C$. Equation (4.1) follows from the definition of asset i's rate of return in different currencies in equation (1.1a). Only if the asset's FX exposure to currency C is 0, the cost of capital conversion is the simpler expression: $1 + k_i^C = \left(1 + k_i^H\right)\left[1 + E^*\left(x^{C/H}\right)\right]$.[1]

Note that we convert an asset's cost of capital <u>not</u> using a managers' actual forecasted rate of FX change, but rather using the expected rate of <u>intrinsic</u> FX change, even if it is different from the managers' FX forecast. The reason is that the cost of capital is a compensation for risk, regardless of the currency perspective. Only the expected rate of <u>intrinsic</u> FX price change is based on systematic risk, and thus preserves a consistent risk and required return relationship across different currencies for a globally traded asset.

Equation (4.1) applies to the hurdle rate for an asset in a developed market, where political risk is ignored. For an emerging market asset, equation (4.1) applies only to the portion of the hurdle rate that is due to the cost of capital and <u>not</u> due to political risk; because a political risk premium has no currency denomination, one would add the political risk premium to the converted cost of capital to get the hurdle rate in currency C.

The tricky aspect of using equation (4.1) is estimating currency H's expected rate of intrinsic FX change versus currency C, $E^*(x^{C/H})$. To estimate $E^*(x^{C/H})$, we'll use the definition of the *currency risk premium* for currency H in terms of currency C, CRP_H^C, as shown in equation (4.2):

Currency Risk Premium

$$CRP_H^C = E^*\left(x^{C/H}\right) + r_f^H - r_f^C \qquad (4.2)$$

As equation (4.2) indicates, if one has an estimate of CRP_H^C, one can get an estimate of $E^*(x^{C/H})$, because r_f^H and r_f^C are observable. To estimate CRP_H^C, we use the ICAPM in equation (2.2), letting asset i be a risk-free deposit in currency H, with required return in currency C of $E(x^{C/H}) + r_f^H$. Thus, the ICAPM estimate for CRP_H^C is equal to $\beta_H^C\left[GRP_1^C\right] + \gamma_H^C\left[XRP_1^C\right]$, where β_H^C is the beta of $x^{C/H}$ versus the global market index in currency C, and γ_H^C is the FX exposure of $x^{C/H}$ to the foreign currency index from the perspective of currency C. Exhibit 4.1 shows ICAPM currency risk premium estimates for the US dollar versus 20 other currencies, based on the 1999 to 2016 data.

For example, let currency C be the euro and currency H be the US dollar. With the 1999 to 2016 data, the percentage changes in the euro per US dollar FX rate had an estimated $\beta_\$^\epsilon$ of 0.155 and $\gamma_\$^\epsilon$ of 1.15, per Exhibit 4.1. With $GRP_1^\epsilon = 5.54\%$ and $XRP_1^\epsilon = -0.92\%$, per Exhibit 2.2, the ICAPM in equation (2.2) yields the currency risk premium estimate of $CRP_\$^\epsilon = 0.155[0.0554] + 1.15[-0.0092] = -0.002$, or -0.20%.

> *Assume that for the US dollar versus the Swiss franc, the standard*
> *risk coefficient estimates are* $\beta_\$^{Sf} = 0.243$ *(versus the global market*
> *index) and* $\gamma_\$^{Sf} = 1.27$ *(versus the foreign currency index), per*
> *Exhibit 4.1. Use the ICAPM equation (2.2) to verify the ICAPM*
> *currency risk premium estimate in Exhibit 4.1 for the US dollar*
> *in terms of the Swiss franc, 0.48%. Assume* $GRP_1^{Sf} = 6.93\%$ *and*
> $XRP_1^{Sf} = -0.95\%$, *per Exhibit 2.2.*
>
> *Answer:* $CRP_\$^{Sf} = 0.243[0.0693] + 1.27[-0.0095] = 0.0048$ *or* 0.48%.

Traditionally, many researchers and analysts have presumed that currency risk premiums are zero, implying the linear version of the traditional uncovered interest rate parity (UIRP) condition: $E^*(x^{C/H}) = r_f^C - r_f^H$. However, you can see in Exhibit 4.1 that currency risk premium estimates are not zero using the ICAPM approach.

Now let's return to the primary tasks of (1) estimating $E^*(x^{\epsilon/\$})$ using an ICAPM currency risk premium estimate; and (2) converting asset i's home-currency cost of capital to an overseas-currency cost of capital. Again, let currency C be the euro and currency H be the US dollar, and so the $CRP_\$^\epsilon$ estimate is -0.20%.

Assume that the risk-free rates are 3% in US dollars and 4% in euros. Using equation (4.2), the estimated equilibrium expected rate of change of the US dollar versus the euro, $E^*(x^{\epsilon/\$})$, is $-0.20\% - 3\% + 4\% = 0.80\%$. Note that 0.80% is not an actual FX forecast, but instead is the percentage FX rate change expected as compensation for both the risk-free rate differential (as in the traditional UIRP condition) and ICAPM FX risk. An $E^*(x^{\epsilon/\$})$ estimate is only a useful forecast if the $\$/\epsilon$ FX rate is correctly valued and expected to remain correctly valued. This idea is analogous to stocks: stock i's cost of equity is not a forecast of an actual expected stock return. Instead, the cost of equity is compensation for

Exhibit 4.1 ICAPM currency risk premium estimates:
US dollar vs. currency C

	$\beta_\$^c$	$\gamma_\$^c$	ICAPM (%)	GCAPM (%)
Global Market Price of Risk = 2.50				
Statistical Parameter Estimation Period: 1999 to 2016				
Eurozone (euro)	0.155	1.15	–0.20	0.79
Japan (yen)	0.273	0.92	1.33	1.98
China (yuan)	–0.003	0.10	–0.05	–0.06
Britain (pound)	0.087	1.11	–0.30	–0.02
Canada (dollar)	–0.080	1.06	–1.27	–0.31
Australia (dollar)	0.159	1.17	–1.38	0.53
Taiwan (dollar)	–0.086	0.76	–0.61	–0.43
Switzerland (franc)	0.243	1.27	0.48	1.45
India (rupee)	–0.041	0.95	–0.80	–0.19
Korea (won)	0.097	1.08	–1.12	0.37
Brazil (real)	0.816	1.02	2.63	5.93
Mexico (peso)	–0.036	0.97	–1.35	0.14
Sweden (krona)	0.130	1.30	–0.82	0.54
Hong Kong (dollar)	–0.001	–0.02	–0.00	0.00
Norway (krone)	0.169	1.25	–0.57	0.77
Denmark Krone)	0.151	1.44	–0.20	0.77
New Zealand (dollar)	0.286	1.16	–0.92	1.10
Singapore (dollar)	–0.081	1.45	–0.61	–0.40
South Africa (rand)	0.495	1.05	–0.37	2.33
Thailand (baht)	0.016	0.93	–0.50	0.08

time (the risk-free rate) and risk, and would be useful as a forecast only if one assumes that the stock is correctly valued and will remain correctly valued.

Finally, assume that asset i has a cost of capital in US dollars of 8% and a FX exposure to the euro of 0.40, and the volatility of $x^{\$/\epsilon}$ is 0.103. Equation (4.1) says that asset i's cost of capital estimate in euros is $(1 + 0.08)[1 + 0.008] - 0.40(0.103)^2 - 1 = 0.0844$, or 8.44%.

After a developed country boxed example for Switzerland, there is an emerging market country boxed example for Mexico, with a political risk premium.

Assume that the currency risk premium for the US dollar versus the Swiss franc is 0.48%, per Exhibit 4.1. Let the US dollar risk-free rate be 3% and the Swiss franc risk-free rate be 2%. A U.S. multinational company has estimated that the cost of capital for its Swiss operation is 10% in US dollars. In US dollars, the operation's FX business exposure to the Swiss franc is 0.50. The volatility of percentage changes in the Swiss franc versus the US dollar FX rate is 0.108. Since the operation is in Switzerland, assume no political risk premium. (a) Use equation (4.2) to find the equilibrium expected rate of change in the US dollar versus the Swiss franc. (b) Find the operation's hurdle rate estimate in Swiss francs.

Answers: (a) $E^*(x^{Sf/\$}) = 0.48\% - 3\% + 2\% = -0.52\%$. (b) $h_{Bi}^{Sf} = k_{Bi}^{Sf} = (1 + 0.10)[1 - 0.0052] - 0.50(0.108)^2 - 1 = 0.0884$, or 8.84%.

Assume that the currency risk premium for the US dollar versus the Mexican peso is −1.35%, per Exhibit 4.1. Let the US dollar risk-free rate be 3% and the Mexican peso risk-free rate be 5%. A U.S. multinational has estimated a hurdle rate for its Mexican operation of 12% in US dollars, including an adjustment for political risk, based on a political risk premium of 0.71% for Mexico, per Exhibit 3.2, and average political risk exposure of 1. The operation's FX business exposure to the Mexican peso is −0.50. The volatility of changes in the Mexican peso versus the US dollar FX rate is 0.096. (a) Use equation (4.2) to find the equilibrium expected rate of change in the US dollar versus the Mexican peso. (b) Find the operation's hurdle rate estimate in Mexican pesos.

Answers: (a) $E^*(x^{Pe/\$}) = -1.35\% - 3\% + 5\% = 0.65\%$. (b) For the cost of capital component (without political risk), $k_{Bi}^{\$} = 0.12 - 1[0.0071] = 0.1129$; therefore, the operation's cost of capital in pesos is $k_{Bi}^{Pe} = (1 + 0.1129)[1 + 0.0065] - (-0.50)(0.096)^2 - 1 = 0.125$, or 12.5%. Adjusting for political risk, the operation's hurdle rate in pesos is: $h_{Bi}^{Pe} = 0.125 + 1[0.0071] = 0.132$, or 13.2%.

Short-Cut Cost of Capital Conversion Practices

The traditional UIRP approach to the intrinsic rate of FX change, and ignoring the interaction between returns and FX changes, has led to simpler "short-cut" cost of capital conversion practices. One approach is to use: $\left(1+k_i^C\right)/\left(1+k_i^H\right)=\left(1+r_f^C\right)/\left(1+r_f^H\right)$. This approach is sometimes an acceptable approximation to the one in equation (4.1), and is easy to apply. An even easier approximation in use, based on the same idea, is: $k_i^C - k_i^H = r_f^C - r_f^H$. In the Swiss franc boxed example problem, we'd get that the k_{Bi}^{Sf} estimate would be $0.02 - 0.03 + 0.10 = 0.09$, or 9%, whereas the ICAPM "correct" answer is 8.84%.

Notice in Exhibit 4.1 that the $CRP_\$^C$ estimate for Australia is the lowest, −1.38%, and the estimate for Brazil is the highest, 2.63%. It is no accident that the global risk premium estimates for the Australian dollar and Brazilian real (in Exhibit 2.2) are 3.29% and 7.28%, respectively, compared to the $GRP^\$$ estimate, 5.92%. That is, a currency's $CRP_\$^C$ estimate is one of the drivers of a currency's global risk premium estimate (in local currency). It is logical that from the perspective of euros, worldwide investors will require a global risk premium that includes a currency risk premium for the uncertainty in the FX price of the US dollar versus the euro, in addition to the global risk premium in US dollars.

The last column in Exhibit 4.1 shows currency risk premium estimates using the GCAPM in currency C, with the global beta for $x^{C/\$}$ and the correct (ICAPM) estimate for GRP^C, per Exhibit 2.2. The average absolute difference between the ICAPM and GCAPM currency risk premium estimates for the US dollar is about 110 basis points. The highest absolute difference is for the Brazilian real (330 basis points), followed by the New Zealand dollar (202 basis points). In general, the GCAPM does <u>not</u> appear to provide a useful approximation to the ICAPM in estimating many currency risk premiums for the US dollar in terms of currency C.

Verify the GCAPM currency risk premium estimate for the US dollar versus the euro, 0.79%, per Exhibit 4.1. Hint: The estimate for $GRP^{€}$ is 5.12%, per Exhibit 2.2.

Answer: With the GCAPM approach, you get $CRP_{\$}^{€} = 0.155[0.0512] = 0.0079$, or 0.79%.

To better understand why the GCAPM does not provide a good approximation to the ICAPM currency risk premium estimates, look at the ICAPM risk coefficient estimates in Exhibit 4.1. The "beta" estimates resemble traditional equity "gamma" estimates, and the "gamma" estimates resemble traditional equity "beta" estimates. That is, whereas equity returns "load" mainly on the market index factor, FX changes are mainly exposed to (load on) the foreign currency index factor, which makes sense. The ICAPM "prices" systematic FX risk separately from systematic market risk and using the foreign currency index risk premium, which is much lower than the global risk premium. So, the GCAPM gives poor approximations to the ICAPM currency risk premium estimates because FX risk in the GCAPM can load only on the market factor and is therefore "priced" with the global risk premium.

Converting Expected Cash Flows

As we said, in the home currency approach to international capital budgeting, a project's expected foreign currency cash flows are converted to equivalent expected home currency cash flows. A standard practice is to simply multiply the expected foreign currency operating cash flow by the expected spot FX rate, expressed in direct terms of the home currency. That is, the standard practice is to find $E\left(O_N^{\$}\right)$ by the product $E\left(O_N^{€}\right) \times E\left(X_N^{\$/€}\right)$, where $E\left(O_N^{€}\right)$ denotes the expected time-N operating cash flow in euros (the representative foreign currency), and $E\left(X_N^{\$/€}\right)$ denotes the expected time-N spot FX rate in US dollars (the representative home currency) per euro.

Technically however, the standard practice is correct <u>only</u> in the special case where the foreign currency cash flow and the spot FX rate are *independent*, which means that the foreign currency cash flow has zero FX operating exposure to the home currency: $\gamma_{OH}^C = 0$. The standard practice calculation does <u>not</u> give the correct expected cash flow in the home currency in the more general situation where the foreign currency cash flow and the FX rate are <u>not</u> independent, that is, when the foreign currency cash flow has a nonzero FX operating exposure to the home currency. Instead, equation (4.3) gives a reasonable approximation to the correct expected time-N cash flow in the home currency, where the US dollar represents the home currency and the euro represents the foreign currency.[2]

Expected Operating Cash Flow Conversion

Home Currency = US Dollar; Foreign Currency = Euro

$$E\left(O_N^{\$}\right) \approx E\left(O_N^{\euro}\right) \times E\left(X_N^{\$/\euro}\right)\left[1 - \gamma_{OS}^{\euro}\left(\sigma_{\euro}^{\$}\right)^2\right]^N \qquad (4.3)$$

Equation (4.3) adjusts the "standard-practice" formula, $E\left(O_N^{\euro}\right) \times E\left(X_N^{\$/\euro}\right)$, by multiplying by the term $\left[1 - \gamma_{OS}^{\euro}(\sigma_{\euro}^{\$})^2\right]^N$, where $\gamma_{OS}^{\euro}$ denotes the foreign project's FX operating exposure to the home currency (the US dollar) and $\left(\sigma_{\euro}^{\$}\right)^2$ denotes the variance (squared volatility) of the annualized percentage changes in the spot FX rate.

For example, assume that Aerotech Components Co. is a U.S. firm considering the acquisition of Vienna Gear Plc., a small aerospace components business in Austria, in the Eurozone. Aerotech expects that under its ownership, Vienna's expected time-1 cash flow in euros, $E(O_1^{\euro})$, would be €10,000. A "what if" analysis shows that the FX operating exposure to the US dollar from the euro point of view, $\gamma_{OS}^{\euro}$, is 0.60.

Assume that the expected time-1 spot FX rate is 1.20 \$/€ and the volatility of the euro (versus the US dollar), $\sigma_{\euro}^{\$}$, is 10.3%, or 0.103 (per annum). Equation (4.3) says that $E(O_1^{\$})$ is (approximately) €10,000(1.20 \$/€)[1 − 0.60(0.103)²] = \$11,924. Using the standard practice of implicitly assuming zero FX exposure to the US dollar, you would get €10,000(1.20 \$/€) = \$12,000, which would *overestimate* the expected time-1 operating cash flow in US dollars.

The U.S. firm Sanders Appliance Co. is considering opening a business operation in England. The English operation is expected to generate operating cash flows of £500,000 per year. Using a "what if" analysis, managers estimated that from the British pound perspective, the operation would have an FX business exposure to the US dollar of 0.80. The volatility of the British pound versus the US dollar is 0.085. Given a forecasted time-1 spot FX rate of 1.50 $/£, find the operation's expected time-1 cash flow in US dollars and compare to the standard practice "estimate."

Answer: Equation (4.3) says that $E(O_1^\$)$ is (approximately) £500,000 (1.50 $/£)[1 − 0.80(0.085)²] = $745,665. Using the standard practice of implicitly assuming zero FX exposure to the US dollar, you would get £500,000(1.50 $/£) = $750,000, which would overestimate the expected time-1 operating cash flow in US dollars.

If the foreign asset's FX exposure to the home currency is negative, the standard practice calculation will *underestimate* the correct expected cash flow in the home currency. The next boxed example demonstrates this point, and relates to the "Illuminating Example" box.

Stanwick Chemical Co. is a U.S. firm considering an acquisition in Brazil that has an FX operating exposure to the US dollar of −0.80. The target's expected time-1 operating cash flow is Re100,000. The expected time-1 spot FX rate is 0.533 $/Re. The volatility of the real is 0.245. (a) Use equation (4.3) to find the approximate expected time-1 operating cash flow in US dollars. (b) Compare the answer in (a) with that of the standard practice approach.

Answers: (a) $E\left(O_1^\$\right) = $ Re100,000(0.533 $/Re)[1 − (−0.80)(0.245)²] = $55,859. (b) Re100,000(0.533 $/Re) = $53,300. Here, the standard practice answer underestimates the equation (4.3) answer because the foreign asset's FX exposure to the home currency is negative.

Illuminating Example

Assume three equally likely outcomes for the time-1 spot FX rate for Brazilian real per US dollar: 1.4 Re/$, 2.0 Re/$, and 2.6 Re/$, with an expected spot FX rate of 2.0 Re/$. In US dollars per Brazilian real, the outcomes are: 0.714 $/Re, 0.50 $/Re, and 0.385 $/Re, with an expected time-1 spot FX rate of (0.714 $/Re + 0.50 $/Re + 0.385 $/Re)/3 = **0.533 $/Re**. From the Brazilian real perspective, the standard deviation of the percentage differences between the spot FX rate outcome and the mean outcome is 0.245. So, we estimate that $\sigma_{Re}^{\$} = 0.245$.

Using a "what if" analysis, if the spot FX rate is 1.40 Re/$, the US dollar is 30% lower than expected. So, given $\gamma_{O\$}^{Re} = -0.80$, the operating cash flow in Brazilian real is higher than expected by 0.80(30%) = 24%, and thus would be 24% higher than Re100,000, or Re124,000. Similarly, if the time-1 spot FX rate is 2.60 Re/$, the US dollar is 30% higher than expected. So, the operating cash flow in Brazilian real would be lower than expected by 24%, and thus would be Re76,000.

Therefore, in US dollars, the actual time-1 operating cash flow will be one of three equally likely outcomes: (1) Re124,000(0.714 $/Re) = $88,536; (2) Re100,000(0.50 $/Re) = $50,000; or (3) Re76,000(0.385 $/Re) = $29,260. The expected time-1 operating cash flow in US dollars is thus ($88,536 + 50,000 + 29,260)/3 = **$55,932**. The approximation in the boxed example using equation (4.3), $55,859, is close to the actual answer, and much closer than the standard practice answer, $53,300.

Probability	$X_1^{Re/\$}$	$X_1^{\$/Re}$	O_1^{Re}	O_1^{Re}
1/3	1.4 Re/$	0.714 $/Re	Re124,000	$88,536
1/3	2.0 Re/$	0.500 $/Re	Re100,000	$50,000
1/3	2.6 Re/$	0.385 $/Re	Re76,000	$29,260
Expected	2.0 Re/$	0.533 $/Re	Re100,000	$55,859

Be sure to see that $\gamma_{O\$}^{\epsilon}$ in equation (4.3) is the euro cash flow's FX exposure to the <u>US dollar</u>, that is, exposure to uncertain changes in the FX price of the US dollar versus the euro. **This exposure is the <u>inverse</u> of the cash flow's FX exposure to the euro from the US dollar perspective, $\gamma_{O\epsilon}^{\$}$, which is used in equation (4.1) to convert an asset's US dollar cost of capital to a euro cost of capital.** Note that the two FX exposure estimates are related as shown in equation (4.4):

FX Exposures: Different Currency Directions

$$\gamma_{O\epsilon}^{\$} + \gamma_{O\$}^{\epsilon} = 1 \tag{4.4}$$

For example, assume that Aerotech Components' analysis of Vienna Gear's FX exposure was easier to conduct from the US dollar perspective. If the "what if" analysis showed that the FX operating exposure to the euro from the US dollar perspective is 0.40, equation (4.4) may be used to find that $\gamma_{O\$}^{\epsilon}$ is $1 - 0.40 = 0.60$, for use in equation (4.3).

Houston Marine Electronics Co. has an Australian operation that has an FX operating exposure to the Australian dollar of 1.40 from the US dollar perspective. Find the operation's FX operating exposure to the US dollar, from the Australian dollar perspective, for use in converting the operation's expected cash flows in Australian dollars to the equivalent expected cash flows in US dollars.

Answer: $\gamma_{O\$}^{A\$} = 1 - 1.40 = -0.40.$

Summary Action Points

- In the home currency approach to cross-border valuation, the analyst converts the expected foreign currency cash flows into home currency equivalents using forecasted FX rates, and then discounts them using a cost of capital denominated in the home currency.

- In the foreign currency approach to cross-border valuation, the analyst converts the home currency cost of capital into an equivalent foreign currency cost of capital and then discounts the expected foreign currency cash flows to get an intrinsic value from the foreign currency perspective.
- The expected rate of intrinsic FX change of one currency versus another is helpful in converting an asset's cost of capital from one currency to another.
- Estimates of the expected rate of intrinsic FX change of one currency versus another may be based on ICAPM currency risk premium estimates.
- The correct conversion of an expected foreign currency cash flow to the home currency often depends on the cash flow's FX exposure and the currency's volatility, and is usually slightly more involved than the simple standard practice of multiplying the expected foreign currency cash flow by the forecasted spot FX price of the foreign currency.

Problems

1. Assume that for the FX rate for the US dollar versus the Korean won, the standard risk coefficient estimates are $\beta_\$^W = 0.097$ (versus the global market index) and $\gamma_\$^W = 1.08$ (versus the foreign currency index), per Exhibit 4.1. Use the ICAPM risk return expression in equation (2.2) to verify the ICAPM currency risk premium estimate in Exhibit 4.1 for the US dollar versus the Korean won, -1.12%. Assume $GRP_1^W = 4.14\%$ and $XRP_1^W = -1.41\%$, per Exhibit 2.2.

2. Assume that the currency risk premium for the US dollar versus the Korean won is -1.12%, per Exhibit 4.1. Let the US dollar risk-free rate be 3% and the Korean won risk-free rate be 2.50%. A U.S. multinational company has estimated a hurdle rate for its Korean operation of 12% in US dollars. In US dollars, the operation's FX business exposure to the Korean won is -0.70. The volatility of percentage changes in the Korean won versus the US dollar FX rate is 0.111. Assume no political risk premium. (a) Use equation (4.2) to find the equilibrium

expected rate of change in the US dollar versus the Korean won. (b) Find the operation's hurdle rate estimate in Korean won.

3. Assume that the currency risk premium for the US dollar versus the Brazilian real is 2.63%, per Exhibit 4.1. Let the risk-free rate be 3% in US dollars and 4% in Brazilian real. A U.S. multinational has estimated a hurdle rate for its Brazilian operation of 16.5% in US dollars, including political risk adjustment of 1.15%, per Exhibit 3.2. The operation's FX business exposure to the Brazilian real is −0.40. The volatility of changes in the Brazilian real versus the US dollar FX rate is 0.245. (a) Use equation (4.2) to find the equilibrium expected rate of change in the US dollar versus the Brazilian real. (b) Find the operation's hurdle rate estimate in Brazilian real.

4. Verify the GCAPM currency risk premium estimate for the US dollar versus the Swiss franc, 1.45%, per Exhibit 4.1. Hint: The estimate for GRP^{sf} is 5.97%, per Exhibit 2.2.

5. The U.S. firm Houston Marine Electronics Co. is considering opening a business operation in Australia. The Australian operation is expected to generate operating cash flows of A$2.5m per year. Using a "what if" analysis, managers estimated that from the Australian dollar perspective, the operation would have an FX business exposure to the US dollar of −0.40, inclusive of an economic "demand effect" of changes in the $/A$ FX rate. The volatility of the Australian dollar versus the US dollar is 0.127. Given a forecasted time-1 spot FX rate of 1.05 $/A$, find the operation's expected time-1 cash flow in US dollars and compare to the standard practice "estimate."

6. A U.S. firm has an operation in the United Kingdom, which has an FX operating exposure to the British pound of 0.20 from the US dollar perspective. Find the operation's FX operating exposure to the US dollar, from the British perspective, for use in converting the operation's expected cash flows in British pounds to the equivalent expected cash flows in US dollars.

Answers to Problems

1. $CRP_\$^{\text{W}} = 0.097[0.0414] + 1.08[-0.0141] = -0.0112$ or -1.12%.

2. a. $E^*\left(x^{\text{W}/\$}\right) = -1.12\% - 3\% + 2.50\% = -1.62\%$.

b. $k_{Bi}^{\cancel{W}} = (1 + 0.12)[1 - 0.0162] - (-0.70)(0.111)^2 - 1$
   $= 0.110 \ (11.0\%)$

3. (a) $E^*(x^{Re/\$}) = 2.63\% - 3\% + 4\% = 3.63\%$. (b) $k_{Bi}^{\$} = 0.165 - 0.0115 = 0.1535$; so, $k_{Bi}^{Re} = (1 + 0.1535)[1 + 0.0363] + 0.40(0.245)^2 - 1 = 0.219$. (b) Adding the political risk adjustment, the operation's hurdle rate in Brazilian real is: $h_{Bi}^{Re} = 0.219 + 0.0115 = 0.231$, or 23.1%.

4. $0.243[0.0597] = 0.0145$, or 1.45%.

5. Equation (4.3) says that $E\left(O_1^{\$}\right)$ is (approximately) A\$2.5m(1.05 \$/A\$) $\times [1 - (-0.40)(0.127)^2] = \$2.642$m. Using the standard practice of implicitly assuming zero FX exposure to the US dollar, you would get A\$2.5m(1.05 \$/A\$) = \$2.625m, which would *underestimate* the expected time-1 operating cash flow in US dollars.

6. $\gamma_{O\$}^{\pounds} = 1 - 0.20 = 0.80$.

Discussion Questions

1. In overseas investment decisions, should one consider the investment's overall cash flow or just the portion to be repatriated? Explain.

2. Zero is a reasonable assumption for a currency risk premium. Discuss.

3. If an asset's cost of capital is 10% in US dollars, the cost of capital will be 10% in any currency or else financial arbitrage would be possible. Evaluate this statement.

4. The expected cash flow in home currency is equal to the product of the expected cash flow in the foreign currency and the expected spot FX price of the foreign currency. Evaluate this statement.

CHAPTER 5

Cross-Border Valuation

Typical textbook advice is that the choice between the home currency and foreign currency approaches is irrelevant in the valuation of an overseas project, and to accept/reject decisions. You will see in this chapter that this advice is based on the implicit assumption that FX rates are correctly valued. That is, the home and foreign currency approaches to cross-border valuation yield consistent results **only if the current and forecasted spot FX rates are <u>intrinsic</u> FX rates (consistent with equilibrium).**

This chapter also shows that if the time-0 spot FX rate is misvalued, or if FX rate forecasts differ from expected intrinsic spot FX rates, the home and foreign currency approaches result in different valuations for the same asset. Thus, NPV analyses in the different currency perspectives may imply different decision outcomes.[1]

For example, if the home currency is overvalued at time 0 versus the foreign currency, a foreign project with a negative NPV in the foreign currency may have a positive NPV from the home currency perspective, because of the windfall FX gain of using an overvalued currency to undertake the investment. Or, if the time-0 spot FX rate is correctly valued but the home currency is forecasted to be overvalued versus the foreign currency in the future, a foreign project with a positive NPV in the foreign currency may have a negative NPV from the home currency perspective, because of the expected windfall FX loss in converting future cash flows from an overvalued foreign currency to the home currency.

Framework for Cross-Border Valuation

Reviewing notation, $E\left(X_N^{\$/€}\right)$ refers to the forecasted <u>actual</u> time-N spot FX rate, and $E^*\left(X_N^{\$/€}\right)$ is the expected <u>intrinsic</u> time-N spot FX rate. Similarly, $X_0^{\$/€}$ denotes the <u>actual</u> time-0 spot FX rate, and $X_0^{*\$/€}$ denotes the <u>intrinsic</u> time-0 spot FX rate. Also, $E\left(x^{\$/€}\right)$ refers to the forecasted rate of <u>actual</u> FX change in the euro versus the US dollar, and $E^{*}\left(x^{\$/\epsilon}\right)$ represents the expected rate of <u>intrinsic</u> FX change in the euro versus the US dollar.

The expected spot FX rate for time N is related to the time-0 spot FX rate and the expected rate of FX change per the relationship shown in equation (5.1).

Expected Spot FX Rate at Time N

$$E\left(X_N^{\$/\epsilon}\right) = X_0^{\$/\epsilon}\left[1 + E\left(x^{\$/\epsilon}\right)\right]^N \tag{5.1}$$

For example, assume the time-0 spot FX rate, $X_0^{\$/\epsilon}$, is 1.21 $/€, and the euro is expected to depreciate by 0.81% versus the US dollar over the next year: $E\left(x^{\$/\epsilon}\right) = -0.81\%$. Then the expected spot FX rate at time 1, $E\left(X_1^{\$/\epsilon}\right)$, is (1.21 $/€)[1 − 0.0081] = 1.20 $/€.

And, because of something called Siegel's paradox, we cannot simply assume that $E\left(x^{\$/C}\right) = -E\left(x^{C/\$}\right)$, or even that $1 + E\left(x^{\$/C}\right) = 1/\left[1 + E\left(x^{C/\$}\right)\right]$. Instead, we need to use the approximation in equation (5.2):[2]

Expected FX Change and Currency Direction

$$E\left(x^{\$/\epsilon}\right) \approx -E\left(x^{\epsilon/\$}\right) + \left(\sigma_\epsilon^{\$}\right)^2 \tag{5.2}$$

For example, assume that the US dollar is expected to appreciate by 1.87% versus the euro, $E\left(x^{\epsilon/\$}\right) = 1.87\%$, and the volatility of $x^{\$/\epsilon}$, $\sigma_\epsilon^{\$}$, is 0.103. (The volatility of $x^{\epsilon/\$}$ and $x^{\$/\epsilon}$ are approximately equal.) Equation (5.2) says that the euro's expected rate of change versus the dollar is $E\left(x^{\$/\epsilon}\right) \approx -0.0187 + (0.103)^2 = -0.0081$, or −0.81%.

The volatility of the Swiss franc versus the US dollar is 0.108. Assume that the expected rate of intrinsic FX change of the US dollar versus the Swiss franc, $E^{*}\left(x^{Sf/\$}\right)$, is 0.58%. Find the expected rate of intrinsic FX change of the Swiss franc versus the US dollar.

Answer: Per equation (5.2), $E^{*}\left(x^{\$/Sf}\right) = -0.0058 + (0.108)^2 = 0.0059$, or 0.59% (approximately).

Exhibit 5.1 Currency Volatility Estimates (versus US Dollar)

Euro	10.3%
Japanese Yen	9.5%
Chinese Yuan	1.7%
British Pound	8.5%
Canadian Dollar	9.1%
Australian Dollar	12.7%
Taiwan Dollar	4.9%
Swiss Franc	10.8%
Indian Rupee	7.3%
Korean Won	11.1%
Brazilian Real	22.6%
Mexican Peso	9.6%
Swedish Krona	11.3%
Hong Kong Dollar	0.4%
Norwegian Krone	11.6%
Denmark Krone	10.2%
New Zealand Dollar	13.5%
Singapore Dollar	5.5%
South African Rand	16.0%
Thai Baht	6.7%

Source: Author's computations using month-end data, 1999 to 2016, from St. Louis Federal Reserve.

Currency volatility estimates are available in many places. Example estimates for some currencies versus the US dollar are shown in Exhibit 5.1.

Cross-Border Valuation and Intrinsic FX Rates

Now let's return to the Aerotech-Vienna Gear example from Chapter 4 and show that the home currency and foreign currency approaches to valuation are equivalent if the FX rates are the intrinsic FX rates. For now, to emphasize the main issues, we assume that Vienna Gear will only be in business for one year, and will generate only next year's operating cash flow, in euros. Vienna Gear's uncertain time-1 cash flow in euros, $O_1^{\euro}$, has an expectation, $E\left(O_1^{\euro}\right)$, of €10,000.

Aerotech's managers have estimated Vienna Gear's cost of capital is 8% in US dollars. That is, $k_B^{\$} = 0.08$. Here is a common scenario where corporate managers have estimated an overseas project's cost of capital in the home currency but have measured the expected operating cash flow stream in the foreign currency. Aerotech has also estimated that in US dollars, Vienna Gear's FX business exposure to the euro, $\gamma_{B\text{€}}^{\$}$, is 0.40.

Let's first apply the foreign currency valuation approach and find Vienna's time-0 intrinsic business value in euros. To do this, we first need to convert Vienna's $k_B^{\$}$ from US dollars to euros, using equation (4.1): $1 + k_i^C = \left(1 + k_i^H\right)\left[1 + E^*\left(x^{C/H}\right)\right] - \gamma_{iC}^H\left(\sigma_C^H\right)^2$. Assume that the risk-free rates are 3% in US dollars and 2.39% in euros, the volatility of the euro versus the US dollar, $\sigma_{\text{€}}^{\$}$, is 0.103, and $E^*\left(x^{\text{€}/\$}\right) = 1.87\%$ (based on equation (4.2) and the ICAPM currency risk premium estimate for the US dollar versus the euro in Exhibit 4.1, −0.20%.) Given that Vienna Gear's $k_B^{\$}$ is 8%, equation (4.1) says that the estimated $k_B^{\text{€}}$ is $(1 + 0.08)$ $[1 + 0.0187] - 0.40(0.103)^2 - 1 = 0.096$, or **9.60%**.

Next, we find Vienna Gear's time-0 intrinsic business value in euros as the present value of the expected future cash flow in euros: $V_B^{\text{€}} = E\left(O_1^{\text{€}}\right)/\left[1 + k_B^{\text{€}}\right] = \text{€}10,000/1.096 = \text{€}9,124$. [In general, $V_i^{\text{€}}$ denotes asset i's intrinsic value in euros. In this case, we know that asset i is the Vienna Gear business operation, so we suppress the i subscript, but use the B subscript to denote the focus on business value.]

We now want to find Vienna Gear's business value from the US dollar (home currency) perspective. For now, assume that Aerotech's managers forecast that the future spot FX rate will be equal to the expected intrinsic spot FX rate. Given this assumption, we'll show that if the parameters of the valuation analysis in each currency are consistent, the present value of the project's expected cash flow in US dollars is equivalent to the present value in euros, given the time-0 <u>intrinsic</u> spot FX rate.

Assume that the time-0 intrinsic spot FX rate, $X_0^{*\$/\text{€}} = \textbf{1.21 \$/€}$. Next, we want to use equation (5.1) to estimate the expected time-1 intrinsic spot FX rate, $E^*(X_1^{\$/\text{€}})$. To do this, we need the expected rate of intrinsic FX change of the euro versus the US dollar, $E^*(x^{\$/\text{€}})$. Given that $E^*(x^{\text{€}/\$}) = 0.0187$ and $\sigma_{\text{€}}^{\$} = 0.103$, equation (5.2) says that $E^*(x^{\$/\text{€}})$ is approximately $-0.0187 + (0.103)^2 = -0.0081$, or **−0.81%**. Then equation (5.1) says that the estimated time-1 intrinsic FX rate is $E^*(X_1^{\$/\text{€}})$ $= (1.21 \text{ \$/€})[1 - 0.0081] = \textbf{1.20 \$/€}$. Since we assume (for now) that the forecasted time-1 <u>actual</u> spot FX rate, $E(X_1^{\$/\text{€}})$, is equal to the expected time-1 intrinsic spot FX rate, the forecasted time-1 <u>actual</u> spot FX rate is also 1.20 $/€.

We are ready to use equation (4.3) to estimate Vienna Gear's expected time-1 operating cash flow in US dollars: $E(O_1^\$)$ is (approximately) €10,000(1.20 $/€)[1 − 0.60(0.103)²] = **$11,924**. Note that we have applied equation (4.4) to convert the FX exposure to the euro, 0.40, to the FX exposure to the US dollar, 0.60.

Since Vienna Gear's cost of capital in US dollars is 8%, the operation's intrinsic business value in US dollars is: $V_B^\$$ = $11,924/1.08 = **$11,041**. This result is the same (except for rounding) as converting the operation's intrinsic business value in euros, **€9,124**, to US dollars at the time-0 intrinsic spot FX rate of 1.21 $/€: $11,040.

A Swiss operation will generate one operating cash flow, expected to be Sf 1,000 at time 1. From the US dollar perspective, the operation's FX operating exposure to the Swiss franc is −0.50 and cost of capital is 10%. The U.S. multinational parent, Enfield Electric Co., owns the Swiss operation and is evaluating an external offer for the operation. The volatility of the Swiss franc versus the US dollar is 0.108. Based on the risk-free rates in US dollars and Swiss francs and the estimated currency risk premium for the US dollar versus the Swiss franc, Enfield's managers estimate the expected rate of intrinsic FX change of the US dollar versus the Swiss franc, $E^*(x^{Sf/\$})$, is 0.58%. Enfield forecasts that the time-1 spot FX rate will be the intrinsic spot FX rate. Assume that the time-0 intrinsic spot FX rate, $X_0^{*Sf/\$}$, is 1 Sf/$. (a) Find the Swiss operation's cost of capital in Swiss francs; (b) Find the operation's intrinsic business value in Swiss francs. (c) Find the expected rate of intrinsic FX change of the Swiss franc versus the US dollar. (d) Find the expected time-1 intrinsic spot FX rate in US dollars per Swiss franc. (e) Find the operation's intrinsic business value in US dollars. (f) Show that the operation's intrinsic business values in Swiss francs and US dollars are equivalent given the time-0 intrinsic spot FX rate.

Answers: (a) Using equation (4.1) k_B^{Sf} = (1 + 0.10)[1 + 0.0058] − (−0.50) (0.108)² − 1 = 0.112, or 11.2%. (b) V_B^{Sf} = Sf1,000/1.112 = Sf 899.

(c) Per equation (5.2), $E^*\left(x^{\$/Sf}\right) = -0.0058 + (0.108)^2 = 0.0059$, or 0.59%. (d) Per equation (5.1), $E^*\left(X_1^{\$/Sf}\right) = 1\ \$/\text{\euro}[1 + 0.0059] = 1.0059\ \$/Sf.$ (e) Because the FX exposure to the Swiss franc is −0.50, the FX exposure to the US dollar is 1.50, per equation (4.4). Using equation (4.3), the operation's expected time-1 operating cash flow in US dollars is $Sf1,000(1.0059\ \$/Sf)[1 − 1.50(0.108)^2] = \$988.$ So, $V_B^{\$} = \$988/1.10 = \$898.$ (f) At the time-0 intrinsic spot FX rate of 1 \$/Sf, $V_B^{Sf} = Sf899$ is (approximately) equivalent to $V_B^{\$} = \$898.$

Now let's bring the project's investment outlay into the analysis. Assume that Vienna Gear's owners are asking **€9,500** for the business. Thus, €9,500 would be Aerotech's investment outlay, viewed in euros, $I^{\text{\euro}}$. Looking at the proposal from the euro point of view, the NPV is $V_B^{\text{\euro}} - I^{\text{\euro}} = \text{\euro}9,124 - 9,500 = -\text{\euro}376.$ That is, **$NPV^{\text{\euro}} = -\text{\euro}376$**. From the euro perspective, the acquisition has a negative NPV, implying rejection of the investment.

Next, we find the NPV in US dollars, if the time-0 <u>actual</u> spot FX rate is 1.21 \$/€ and is thus correctly valued. Aerotech's investment outlay from the US dollar perspective, $I^{\$}$, would thus be 1.21 \$/€(€9,500) = **\$11,495**. Therefore, the NPV in US dollars is \$11,040 − 11,495 = −\$455. That is, **$NPV^{\$} = -\$455$**. The $NPV^{\$}$ is equivalent to $NPV^{\text{\euro}}$ at the time-0 spot FX rate, because −€376(1.21 \$/€) = −\$455.

In this example with correctly-valued (intrinsic) FX rates, the two currency perspectives lead to equivalent NPV amounts, given that the inputs to the analysis are consistent across the currencies. Thus, the two currency perspectives imply the same decision outcome. In principle, it does not matter which currency is chosen for the NPV analysis, because you reach the same accept/reject decision by conducting the NPV analysis in euros, with a euro cost of capital and an expected euro cash flow, or in US dollars, with a US dollar cost of capital and an expected cash flow converted from euros into US dollars.

You will sometimes see this irrelevance conclusion stated as a general proposition with the implication that it always holds. As you will see next, however, that generalization is incorrect. **The home and foreign currency approaches to international investments give equivalent NPVs _only if_ the FX rates are the intrinsic FX rates.**

Misvalued Time-0 Spot FX Rate

Next, we look at a scenario where the euro is *undervalued* versus the US dollar at time 0, but the FX rate is expected to be correctly valued in the future.[3] For a given time-0 investment outlay in euros, the undervaluation of the euro at time 0 implies that the project's $NPV^\$$ will be higher than the US dollar equivalent of $NPV^\euro$, given the time-0 <u>actual</u> spot FX rate.

Assume that the time-0 <u>actual</u> spot FX rate is $X_0^{\$/\euro} = 1$ $/€, whereas the time-0 intrinsic spot FX rate is 1.21 $/€. Aerotech's investment outlay from the US dollar perspective is 1 $/€(€9,500) = $9,500. That is, $I^\$ = $9,500$. Vienna Gear's $V_B^\$$ is not affected by the time-0 spot FX misvaluation, given that the FX forecast is still the expected time-1 intrinsic spot FX rate, 1.20 $/€. That is, $V_B^\$$ is still $11,924/1.08 = $11,040, regardless of the time-0 spot FX rate. So $NPV^\$ = $11,040 − 9,500 = $1,540$. That is, $NPV^\$ = $1,540$.

Note that even though the $NPV^\$$ <u>is</u> affected by whether the time-0 actual spot FX rate is correctly valued, the $NPV^\euro$ is <u>not</u> affected. Regardless of the time-0 actual spot FX rate, $NPV^\euro = €9,124 − 9,500 = −€376$. So, we see that the two NPVs are <u>not</u> necessarily equivalent to each other when the time-0 spot FX rate is misvalued. Indeed, in this example, it matters for the accept/reject decision which currency is chosen for the NPV analysis, because the project's NPV in euros is negative and the NPV in US dollars is positive. A <u>reject decision</u> is implied by $NPV^\euro$, but an <u>accept decision</u> is implied by $NPV^\$$.

In this example, the FX market conditions allow Aerotech to convert US dollars into euros for the investment outlay at time 0 at a "bargain" spot FX rate, yet expect to convert the acquisition's future cash flow at a correctly valued future spot FX rate. The time-0 spot FX misvaluation is temporary and forecasted to be corrected by time 1. The box on Toronto-Dominion Bank, October 2007 is a real-world example where the home currency is overvalued versus the foreign currency at time 0.

Toronto-Dominion Bank, October 2007

"Helped by the strength of the Canadian dollar, TORONTO-DOMINION BANK agreed to buy COMMERCE BANCORP, an American retail bank, for $8.5 billion in October 2007. The deal cemented the Canadian bank's presence in America's north-east."

This news quote suggests that the FX rate played a role in this acquisition decision. Perhaps the "strength of the Canadian dollar" was a view that the Canadian dollar was overvalued and the US dollar undervalued, at that time. Such an FX misvaluation may have implied that the acquisition of COMMERCE BANCORP would have a positive NPV to TORONTO-DOMINION BANK. If the Canadian dollar had been correctly valued, the acquisition may not have had a positive NPV.

It is relatively easy to think of an example of the opposite situation, where the foreign currency (euro) is *overvalued* versus the home currency (US dollar) at time 0, and the acquisition's $NPV^{€}$ is positive, but the $NPV^{\$}$ is negative. For example, assume that Vienna Gear's owners are only asking €8,500 for the business and that the time-0 actual spot FX rate is 1.40 $/€. The acquisition has a positive $NPV^{€}$: €9,124 − 8,500 = €624. But in US dollars, the outlay for the acquisition is 1.40 $/€(€8,500) = $11,900. So, the $NPV^{\$}$ is negative, $11,040 − 11,900 = −$860.

Extend the previous Enfield Electric example problem. Enfield has been offered Sf 800 for the Swiss operation. Assume that the time-0 actual spot FX rate, in direct terms from the US dollar perspective, is 1.25 $/Sf, even though the time-0 intrinsic spot FX rate is 1 $/Sf. So, the Swiss franc is overvalued versus the US dollar at time 0. Enfield believes that the time-0 overvaluation of the Swiss franc is temporary and will be corrected before the Swiss operation's time-1 cash flow. Find the NPV to Enfield of selling the Swiss operation, in Swiss francs and in US dollars.

Answer: When compared to the Swiss operation's intrinsic business value of Sf 899, the offer of Sf 800 represents a loss in Swiss francs to Enfield, −Sf 99. (The operation's buyer would gain Sf 99, if Enfield were to accept the offer.) Since the offer of Sf 800 converts to $1,000 at the actual spot FX rate, selling the operation for $1,000 when the business value is $899 has is a gain of $101 to Enfield. Enfield gets a windfall FX gain by selling the Swiss operation when the Swiss franc is overvalued versus the US dollar. In this case, the windfall FX gain is more than enough to offset the Sf 99 loss in business value.

Forecasts of Misvalued Future FX Rates

This section extends the analysis to the case where the managers' actual forecast of a future FX rate differs from the expected intrinsic FX rate. As you might suspect, the two present values of expected cash flows will not be equivalent across the currency perspectives, even converting with the time-0 intrinsic spot FX rate.[4]

Let's pick up the Aerotech/Vienna Gear example and assume again that the expected time-1 intrinsic spot FX rate is 1.20 $/€, but that Aerotech's managers' forecast for the <u>actual</u> time-1 spot FX rate is 1.30 $/€. That is, $E^*\left(X_1^{\$/€}\right)$ = 1.20 $/€ and $E\left(X_1^{\$/€}\right)$ = **1.30 $/€**. In this scenario, the euro is expected to be overvalued versus the US dollar when the project's cash flow is received at time 1. If the time-0 spot FX rate is correctly valued, the forecast for the euro to be overvalued at time 1 implies that the project's $NPV^{\$}$ will be higher than the US dollar equivalent of $NPV^{€}$.

Vienna Gear's actual expected cash flow, measured in US dollars, is $E(O_1^{\$})$ = €10,000(1.30 $/€)[1 − 0.60(0.103)²] = **$12,917**. To correctly value the operation in US dollars, we need to break down $E(O_1^{\$})$ into two components. The first component is the expected cash flow given the expected time-1 *intrinsic* spot FX rate (1.20 $/€), which we already know is **$11,924**. We'll call this component the intrinsic expected cash flow, $E^*(O_1^{\$})$. The second component is simply the difference between the actual expected cash flow and the intrinsic expected cash flow, $E(O_1^{\$}) − E^*(O_1^{\$})$, which is $12,917 − 11,924 = **$993**.

The reason for breaking $E(O_1^{\$})$ into two components is that we need to discount the components at different rates, because of the different systematic risks. We need to discount the intrinsic expected cash flow component at Vienna Gear's cost of capital in US dollars, 8%, which is based on the operation's systematic business risk. We already know that the present value of this component is $11,924/1.08 = **$11,040**.

Since the expected cash flow's second component, the FX windfall of $993, is due solely to FX market conditions and not business risk, we need to discount the second component at a required rate of return that reflects the <u>systematic FX risk</u> of the euro versus US dollar FX rate. Therefore, the correct discount rate for the FX windfall component is the required rate of return in US dollars on a one-year risk-free euro deposit. The deposit pays the risk-free rate in euros, $r_f^{\mathrm{\euro}}$, and in equilibrium, the investor also gets the risk compensation of $E^*\left(x^{\$/\mathrm{\euro}}\right)$. Therefore, a US dollar investor's required rate of return on a euro deposit, $k_{\mathrm{\euro}}^{\$} = r_f^{\mathrm{\euro}} + E^*\left(x^{\$/\mathrm{\euro}}\right)$, is the correct discount rate for expected FX windfall cash-flow components, as shown in equation (5.3).

Discount Rate for FX Windfall Component

$$k_{\mathrm{\euro}}^{\$} = r_f^{\mathrm{\euro}} + E^*\left(x^{\$/\mathrm{\euro}}\right) \tag{5.3}$$

As we assumed earlier that $r_f^{\mathrm{\euro}} = 2.39\%$ and $E^*\left(x^{\$/\mathrm{\euro}}\right) = -0.81\%$, the required rate of return in US dollars on a one-year risk-free euro deposit is $2.39\% - 0.81\% = 1.58\%$. Therefore, the present value of the expected FX windfall component equals $\$993/1.0158 = \mathbf{\$978}$. Adding the component present values, the value of the $\$12,917$ actual expected time-1 cash flow is $\$11,040 + 978 = \mathbf{\$12,018}$. That is, Vienna Gear's intrinsic business value in US dollars is $\$12,018$.

So, you see that if one forecasts a future spot FX rate that is NOT the expected intrinsic spot FX rate, the present value of the expected cash flows is NOT equivalent for the two currency choices, even with conversion at the time-0 intrinsic spot FX rate. If you convert the US dollar cost of capital to euros, find the present value in euros, and then convert the present value to US dollars using the time-0 intrinsic spot FX rate, you get $\$11,040$. If you convert the expected euro cash flow to US dollars at the forecasted actual time-1 spot FX rate, the intrinsic business value is $\$12,018$. If the outlay for the project were $\$11,500$, the project would have a negative NPV from the euro perspective but a positive NPV from the US dollar perspective because of the forecasted time-1 overvaluation of the euro versus the US dollar.

Extend the previous Enfield Electric example problems. Assume that the time-0 actual spot FX rate is equal to the intrinsic spot FX rate, 1 $/Sf. Enfield's managers forecast a time-1 actual spot FX rate of 1.20 $/Sf, whereas the expected time-1 intrinsic spot FX rate is 1.0059 $/Sf. Assume that the Swiss franc risk-free rate is 3.10%.

A U.S. company has offered $1,000 to Enfield for the Swiss oper-
ation. (a) Find the NPV in Swiss francs to Enfield of the proposed
sale. (b) Find the actual expected operating cash flow in US dollars
and the two components. (c) Find the required rate of return on a
1-year risk-free Swiss franc deposit. (d) Find the NPV to Enfield in
US dollars of the proposed sale.

Answers: (a) In Swiss francs, Enfield would gain Sf101 by selling the oper-
ation for Sf1000 when it's only worth Sf899; NPV = Sf1,000 − 899 =
Sf101. (b) The actual expected time-1 operating cash flow in US dollars
is Sf1,000(1.20 $/Sf)[1 − 1.50(0.108)²] = $1,179. The intrinsic compo-
nent is Sf1,000(1.0059 $/Sf)[1 − 1.50(0.108)²] = $988, as before. So,
the FX windfall component is $1,179 − 988 = $191. (c) Since the Swiss
franc risk-free rate is 3.10% and the intrinsic rate of FX change of the
Swiss franc versus the US dollar is 0.59%, the required rate of return on
the Swiss franc risk-free deposit is 3.10% + 0.59% = 3.69%, per equa-
tion (5.3). (d) $V_B^\$$ = $988/1.10 + 191/1.0369 = $898 + 184 = $1,082.
Selling the Swiss operation for $1,000 when the operation has an intrinsic
value in US dollars of $1,082 would imply a loss to Enfield: NPV =
$1,000 − 1,082 = −$82. Enfield should not sell the Swiss operation for
$1,000, because Enfield expects to receive a time-1 cash flow that will be
converted at an overvalued FX price of the Swiss franc.

Multiperiod Cash Flows

This section tackles the more common scenario of multiperiod cash flows. We examine the case where the analyst forecasts the foreign currency to be misvalued for multiple periods. For this scenario, we use a "short-cut" that involves converting the present value of the expected operating cash flows in euros to US dollars using the time-0 intrinsic spot FX rate.

To establish the "short-cut" method, note first that if forecasted future spot FX rates are equal to the expected intrinsic spot FX rates, the home currency present value of a foreign project's future expected cash flows is equal to foreign currency present value of the project's future expected cash flows times the time-0 intrinsic spot FX rate, $X_0^{*\$/€}\left(V_B^€\right)$.

Each period's expected FX windfall may be found using the difference between the actual forecasted FX rate and the expected intrinsic FX rate: $O_N^\mathcal{\euro} \left[E(X_N^{\$/\euro}) - E^*(X_N^{\$/\euro}) \right] \left[1 - \gamma_{O\$}^\mathcal{\euro} (\sigma_\mathcal{\euro}^\$)^2 \right]^N$. Let $V_{FX}^\$$ denote the present value of the expected FX windfall components. Then a foreign operation's intrinsic business value in the home currency is given in equation (5.4).

Intrinsic Business Value in US Dollars

$$V_B^\$ = X_0^{*\$/\euro} \left(V_B^\mathcal{\euro} \right) + V_{FX}^\$ \tag{5.4}$$

For example, say Vienna Gear will generate five years of euro cash flows, with the expected cash flow being €10,000 each year. Still assume that the operation's cost of capital in US dollars is 8%, the FX operating exposure to the euro is 0.40, the volatility of the euro versus the US dollar is 0.103, $E^*\left(x^{\$/\euro}\right) = -0.81\%$, $k_\mathcal{\euro}^\$ = 1.58\%$, and the time-0 intrinsic spot FX rate, $X_0^{*\$/\euro}$, is 1.21 $/€. So, the operation's cost of capital in euros is still 9.60%. The intrinsic business value in euros is $V_B^\mathcal{\euro} = €10,000/1.096 + 10,000/1.096^2 + 10,000/1.096^3 + 10,000/1.096^4 + 10,000/1.096^5 = €38,298$.

Exhibit 5.2 shows the expected intrinsic future FX rates, based on $E^*\left(x^{\$/\euro}\right) = -0.81\%$ and $X_0^{*\$/\euro} = 1.21$ $/€. Assume that Aerotech's managers forecast that the time-1 FX rate will be 1.30 $/€, and that the euro's forecasted overvaluation will gradually dissipate to the correct FX valuation by year 5, 1.16 $/€, per Exhibit 5.2. Exhibit 5.2 shows the operation's expected FX windfall cash flows in US dollars, found using the short-cut described previously.

Exhibit 5.2 5-Year FX Windfall Cash Flows

N	$E(X_N^{\$/\euro})$	$E^*(X_N^{\$/\euro})$	$O_N^\mathcal{\euro} [E(X_N^{\$/\euro}) - E^*(X_N^{\$/\euro})][1 - \gamma_{O\$}^\mathcal{\euro}(\sigma_\mathcal{\euro}^\$)^2]^N$
1	1.30 $/€	1.20 $/€	$994
2	1.26 $/€	1.19 $/€	$691
3	1.22 $/€	1.18 $/€	$392
4	1.19 $/€	1.17 $/€	$195
5	1.16 $/€	1.16 $/€	0

The present value of the expected FX windfall cash flows, $V_{FX}^{\$}$, is $\$994/1.0158 + 691/1.0158^2 + 392/1.0158^3 + 195/1.0158^4 = \$2,205$. Per equation (5.4), Aerotech's estimate of the investment's intrinsic business value in US dollars is $(1.21 \ \$/€)€38,298 + \$2,205 = \textbf{\$48,546}$.

The Austrian firm Luna Instruments will generate uncertain future operating cash flows, expected to be €1m per year perpetually. The U.S. multinational company, Olympic Machine Tools, is considering the acquisition of Luna. Olympic estimates that from the US dollar perspective, Luna's FX operating exposure to the euro is 1.50 (so the FX exposure to the US dollar is −0.50), and the cost of capital in US dollars is 9%. Assume: the euro risk-free rate is 2.39%; the volatility of the $/€ FX rate is 0.103; $E^{*}(x^{\$/€}) = -0.81\%$, and $E^{*}(x^{€/\$}) = 1.87\%$; and the time-0 intrinsic and actual spot FX rates are 1.21 $/€ and 1.11 $/€, respectively. Olympic forecasts that the spot FX rate will gradually converge to the expected intrinsic spot FX rate by year 5, as follows: $E(X_1^{\$/€}) = 1.12 \ \$/€$; $E(X_2^{\$/€}) = 1.13 \ \$/€$; $E(X_3^{\$/€}) = 1.14 \ \$/€$; $E(X_4^{\$/€}) = 1.15 \ \$/€$. (a) Find Luna's intrinsic business value in euros. (b) Make a table in the format of Exhibit 5.2. (c) Find Olympic's estimate of Luna's intrinsic business value in US dollars.

Answers: (a) Per equation (4.1), $k_B^{€} = (1 + 0.09)[1 + 0.0187] - 1.50(0.103)^2 - 1 = 0.0945$, or 9.45%. $V_B^{€} = €1m/0.0945 = €10.6m$.

(b)

N	$E(X_N^{\$/€})$	$E^{*}(X_N^{\$/€})$	$O_N^{€}[E(X_N^{\$/€}) - E^{*}(X_N^{\$/€})] \times$ $[1 - \gamma_{0\$}^{€}(\sigma_{€}^{\$})^2]^N$
1	1.12 $/€	1.20 $/€	−$0.08m
2	1.13 $/€	1.19 $/€	−$0.06m
3	1.14 $/€	1.18 $/€	−$0.04m
4	1.15 $/€	1.17 $/€	−$0.02m
5	1.16 $/€	1.16 $/€	

(c) $V_{FX}^{\$} = -\$0.08m/1.0158 - \$0.06m/1.0158^2 - \$0.04m/1.0158^3 - \$0.02m/1.0158^4 = -\$0.194m$. Per equation (5.4), $V_B^{\$} = (1.21 \ \$/€)€10.6m - \$0.194m = \$12.6m$.

Debate: Foreign Versus Home
Currency Valuation Approaches

We have seen that the home and foreign currency approaches give equivalent NPVs with intrinsic FX rates, but not with any time-0 or forecasted FX misvaluation. The home currency approach incorporates the FX misvaluation, whereas the foreign currency approach does not. Which approach should you use?

Some think that an investment decision should <u>not</u> consider expected windfall FX gains and losses and thus that the foreign currency NPV indicates the correct investment decision. Proponents of this approach make two arguments. The first is that managers do not know enough about FX rates to have informed FX valuation opinions and forecasts, and so the managers should stick to managing their business instead of trying to estimate intrinsic FX values and forecast FX rates.

Second, even if managers could reliably judge intrinsic FX values and forecast FX rates, they could better exploit their judgments by using a financial market transaction instead of a business investment. To see this point, consider the Vienna Gear scenario where the euro is undervalued versus the US dollar at time 0, but the FX rate is forecasted to be correctly valued by time 1. Instead of acquiring Vienna Gear, Aerotech would be better off to invest the $9,500 in a risk-free euro deposit, paying $9,500 for an asset that is intrinsically worth $11,495, for an NPV of $1,995. Acquiring Vienna Gear, with a US dollar NPV of $1,540, should be rejected in favor of the euro deposit with an NPV of $1,995. In other words, why package the business investment together with an FX speculation when the FX speculation by itself is better?

A different school of thought favors the home currency approach <u>because</u> the foreign currency NPV ignores the windfall FX gains/losses. Proponents of this approach argue that if managers have an informed view on FX rates, why should they ignore this information when making investment decisions? Maybe the managers' FX information comes from FX research experts of a top-notch FX forecasting service.

Second, a financial market transaction like a euro deposit is usually not a realistic alternative to a business investment. For one thing, acquiring Vienna Gear is consistent with Aerotech's business, but speculating in a euro deposit is not. That is, FX speculation may be frowned-upon on its own, but may be "OK" if embedded in a business decision. For another thing, managers are likely to want to avoid the volatility that the mark-to-market (MTM) changes in the euro deposit would create in reported earnings. From Aerotech's home currency perspective, acquiring Vienna Gear adds less value than investing in a euro deposit, but acquiring Vienna Gear may still be a more practical way for Aerotech's managers to add value, given a view that the euro is currently undervalued versus the US dollar and their forecast that the current FX misvaluation will be corrected by time 1.

On one point, there is agreement: If a company wants to manage an overseas investment's FX operating exposure with financial hedging, say with foreign currency debt, this tactic has its own windfall FX effects that will tend to offset the FX windfall effects of the investment. It seems plausible that an optimal level of financial hedging would trade off the hedging benefit of lower financial distress costs with the nonhedging benefit of capturing windfall FX gains. A model of this type is beyond our scope. Another consideration is if the company already has some natural short exposure to the foreign currency that will serve as an operational hedge. If so, then financial hedging of the FX operating exposure of a proposed investment is less needed, and a new project with a predicted windfall FX gain might be acceptable.

The debate is difficult to resolve, because both sides make reasonable points. Assessing whether a spot FX rate is misvalued is difficult even for economists, let alone managers. Yet we often see opinions and forecasts from major global banks and other financial services about FX misvaluation. And both sides make good points about the "bundling" of a corporate investment with FX speculation.

Academic researchers have empirically studied whether foreign direct investment (FDI) relates to spot FX rates, but the evidence is inconclusive, particularly on how FDI relates to FX misvaluations.[5]

So, the choice is yours: **use the home currency approach if you want to incorporate a view on FX misvaluation in the NPV analysis, or use the foreign currency approach if you want to avoid doing so.**

Summary Action Points

- The conventional view is that an asset's intrinsic value will be the same in one currency as in another, given the spot FX rate. Similarly, it is often asserted that it is irrelevant whether we analyze a foreign project's NPV in the home currency or the foreign currency, if consistent cross-border cash flow forecasts and costs of capital are used. These assertions implicitly assume correctly valued FX rates.
- Given an FX misvaluation, the choice of currency perspective of the NPV analysis is relevant, due to expected windfall FX gains or losses.
- The home currency approach to cross-border valuation incorporates the windfall FX gains and losses, whereas the foreign currency approach does not. In this environment, managers' FX valuation and forecasts might affect their overseas investment decisions.

Glossary

Foreign Currency Approach (to Cross-Border Valuation): The analyst discounts the expected cash flows denominated in the foreign currency using a cost of capital denominated in the foreign currency.

Home Currency Approach (to Cross-Border Valuation): The analyst converts the expected foreign currency cash flows into home currency equivalents using forecasted FX rates, and then discounts them using a cost of capital denominated in the home currency.

Problems

For 1 to 8: The U.S. multinational Southwest Materials Co. is evaluating a Swedish acquisition target that will generate a single operating cash flow, one year from now, expected to be Sk10m. From the US dollar perspective, the target's FX operating exposure to the Swedish krona is 1.50. The target's private equity owner is asking Sk9m for the operation.

Southwest has estimated the target's cost of capital (and hurdle rate) is 10% in US dollars. Southwest forecasts that the future spot FX rate will be the intrinsic spot FX rate. The volatility of the Swedish krona versus the US dollar = 0.113; the time-0 intrinsic spot FX rate = 6.25 Sk/$; the US dollar risk-free rate is equal to the krona risk-free rate, 3%; and the equilibrium expected rate of intrinsic FX change in the US dollar versus the krona is −0.82%.

1. Estimate the equilibrium expected rate of change of the krona versus the US dollar. Hint: use equation (5.2).
2. Determine the forecasted time-1 FX rate in $/Sk.
3. Find the expected cash flow in US dollars.
4. Estimate the cost of capital for the Swedish target in Swedish kronor.
5. Estimate the intrinsic business value of the Swedish target in kronor.
6. Estimate the intrinsic business value of the Swedish target in US dollars.
7. Find the NPV of the Swedish target in US dollars if the actual time-0 spot FX rate is the intrinsic spot FX rate, 6.25 Sk/$.
8. Estimate the NPV of the Swedish target in US dollars if the krona is overvalued in the time-0 spot FX market because the actual spot FX rate is 5 Sk/$.

For 9 to 11: The British firm Bristol Tools Ltd. will generate one uncertain British pound operating cash flow, expected to be £1m at time 1. In US dollars, Bristol's FX operating exposure to the British pound is 0.70 and cost of capital is 9%. Deck and Blacker Company, a U.S. multinational, owns Bristol Tool. The time-0 actual spot FX rate is 1.60 $/£, but Deck and Blacker's managers believe that the time-0 intrinsic spot FX rate is 1.50 $/£. The managers also believe that the British pound's time-0 overvaluation versus the US dollar will be corrected by time 1 and thus that the time-1 spot FX rate will be the intrinsic spot FX rate. The volatility of the British pound versus the US dollar is 0.085, and the equilibrium expected rate of intrinsic FX change in the US dollar versus the pound is 1.32%. Deck and Blacker's managers want to indicate an asking price in British pounds that would give the buyer a positive NPV in pounds and Black and Decker a positive NPV in US dollars.

9. (a) Estimate Bristol's intrinsic business value in British pounds. (b) What is the forecasted (intrinsic) time-1 spot FX rate? (c) Find Bristol's intrinsic business value in US dollars. (d) Confirm that the intrinsic business values in British pounds and US dollars are equivalent at the time-0 intrinsic spot FX rate.

10. Deck and Blacker indicates an initial asking price of £900,000. (a) For a British pound buyer, what would be the acquisition's NPV in British pounds? (b) What would be the sale's NPV in US dollars to Deck and Blacker?

11. Assume that Deck and Blacker change their forecast for the time-1 FX rate to 1.55 $/£. Assume that the British pound risk-free rate is 4.62%. Find the NPV in US dollars to Deck and Blacker if it sells Bristol Tool for £900,000.

For 12 to 14: A U.S. multinational expects its Swiss operation to generate Sf 2,000 per year in operating cash flow perpetually. The multinational estimates that in US dollars, the operation's FX operating exposure to the Swiss franc is −0.50 and the cost of capital is 10%. Assume that the US dollar and Swiss franc risk-free rates are 3% and 3.10%, respectively; and $E^*\left(x^{Sf/\$}\right) = 0.58\%$ and $E^*\left(x^{\$/Sf}\right) = 0.59\%$. The volatility of the $/Sf FX rate changes is 0.108. The time-0 actual and intrinsic spot FX rates are 1.25 $/Sf and 1 $/Sf. Managers forecast that the actual spot FX rate will gradually converge to the intrinsic spot FX rate by year 5, as follows: $E\left(X_1^{\$/Sf}\right) =$ 1.20 $/Sf; $E\left(X_2^{\$/Sf}\right) = 1.15$ $/Sf; $E\left(X_3^{\$/Sf}\right) = 1.10$ $/Sf; $E\left(X_4^{\$/Sf}\right) =$ 1.05 $/Sf.

12. Find the Swiss operation's intrinsic business value in Swiss francs.

13. Make a table in the format of Exhibit 5.2.

14. Find the Swiss operation's intrinsic business value in US dollars.

Answers to Problems

1. Using equation (5.2), the equilibrium expected rate of change of the krona versus the US dollar is approximately $-(-0.0082) + (0.113)^2 =$ 0.021, or 2.10%.

2. Using equation (5.1), the expected time-1 intrinsic spot FX price of the krona is (0.16 $/Sk)[1.021] = 0.163 $/Sk.

3. Using equation (4.3), the expected operating cash flow in US dollars is Sk10m(0.163 \$/Sk)[1 − (−0.50)(0.113)^2] = \$1.65m.

4. Using equation (4.1), the operation's cost of capital in Swedish kronor is 1.10[1 − 0.0082] − 1.50(0.113)^2 − 1 = 0.0718, or 7.18%

5. The intrinsic business value in kronor is Sk10m/1.0718 = Sk9.33m.

6. The intrinsic business value in US dollars \$1.65m/1.10 = \$1.50m. We get approximately the same answer by converting the intrinsic business value in kronor to US dollars at the time-0 intrinsic FX rate: (0.16 \$/Sk)(Sk9.33m) = \$1.49m.

7. $I^\$$ = Sk9m/(6.25 Sk/\$) = \$1.44m. $NPV^\$$ = \$1.50m − 1.44m = \$0.06m, or \$60,000.

8. $I^\$$ = Sk9m/(5 Sk/\$) = \$1.80m. $NPV^\$$ = \$1.50m − 1.80m = −\$0.30m.

9. (a) Bristol's cost of capital in British pounds is 1.09[1.0132] − 0.70(0.085)^2 − 1 = 0.0993, or 9.93%. Bristol's intrinsic business value in British pounds is £1m/1.0993 = £0.91m.

   (b) Using equation (5.2), the equilibrium expected change in the British pound versus the US dollar is approximately −0.0132 + (0.085)^2 = −0.006, or −0.6%. The expected time-1 FX rate is 1.50 \$/£(1 − 0.006) = 1.491 \$/£.

   (c) The expected time-1 operating cash flow in US dollars is approximately £1m(1.491 \$/£)[1 − 0.30(0.085)^2] = \$1.49m. Bristol's intrinsic business value in US dollars is \$1.49m/1.09 = \$1.37m.

   (d) At the time-0 intrinsic spot FX rate of 1.50 \$/£, Bristol's intrinsic business value in British pounds, £0.91m is equivalent to the intrinsic business value in US dollars, \$1.37m, because £0.91m(1.50 \$/£) = \$1.37m.

10. (a) £91m − 0.90m = £0.01m, or £10,000.

    (b) £0.90m(1.60 \$/£) − \$1.37m = \$0.07m, or \$70,000.

11. 1.58 \$/£ − 1.491 \$/£ = 0.089 \$/£. The expected time-1 FX windfall to Deck and Blacker from owning Bristol is £1m(0.089 \$/£)[1 − 0.30(0.085)^2] = \$0.089m. Applying equation (5.2), the discount rate in US dollars for the FX windfall is 0.0462 − 0.006 = 0.0402. The present value of the FX windfall = \$0.089m/1.0402 = \$0.086m. The intrinsic business value in US dollars is \$1.37m + 0.086m = \$1.456m. Selling for £0.90m would be an $NPV^\$$ equal to £0.90m(1.60 \$/£) − 1.456m = −\$0.016m, or −\$16,000. If Deck and Blacker forecasts a

time-1 overvaluation of the British pound versus the US dollar, the sale is not advantageous, even though the time-0 sale would also be at a time when the pound is overvalued versus the US dollar.

12. Using equation (4.1) $k_B^{Sf} = (1+0.10)[1+0.0058] - (-0.50)(0.108)^2 - 1 = 0.112$, or 11.2%. V_B^{Sf} is Sf 2,000/0.112 = Sf 17,857.

13.

N	$E\left(X_N^{\$/Sf}\right)$	$E^*\left(X_N^{\$/Sf}\right)$	$O_N^{Sf}\left[E\left(X_N^{\$/Sf}\right)-E^*\left(X_N^{\$/Sf}\right)\right]\times$ $\left[1-\gamma_{Os}^{Sf}\left(\sigma_{Sf}^{\$}\right)^2\right]^N$
1	1.20 $/Sf	1.006 $/Sf	$381
2	1.15 $/Sf	1.012 $/Sf	$266
3	1.10 $/Sf	1.018 $/Sf	$156
4	1.05 $/Sf	1.023 $/Sf	$ 50
5	1.029 $/Sf	1.029 $/Sf	0

14. With the expected intrinsic spot FX rates, the intrinsic business value in US dollars is Sf 17,857(1 $/Sf) = $17,857. Per equation (5.2), $E^*\left(x^{\$/Sf}\right) = -0.0058 + (0.108)^2 = 0.0059$, or 0.59%. Since 3.10% + 0.59% = 3.69% is the required return in US dollars on a risk-free Swiss franc deposit, the present value in US dollars of the expected FX windfalls is $381/1.0369 + $266/1.0369^2 + $156/1.0369^3 + $50/1.0369^4 = $798. So, $V_B^{\$} = $17,857 + 798 = $18,655.

Discussion Questions

1. Discuss situations where managers should consider the level of FX rates in overseas investment analysis.

2. Discuss situations where managers should not consider the level of FX rates in overseas investment analysis.

3. Do you think managers incorporate their FX forecasts into international investment decisions?

4. Do you think managers *should* incorporate their FX forecasts into international investment decisions?

CHAPTER 6

International Capital Budgeting Applications

The previous chapter's coverage of cross-border valuation featured two basic types of international capital budgeting applications: the acquisition and sale of a foreign operation. This chapter looks at some additional international capital budgeting scenarios: (a) a plant modernization proposal by an overseas subsidiary; and (b) a proposal to relocate some or all of production from the home country to a foreign country, or vice versa, considering possible changes in political risk or FX operating exposure. The relocation scenarios may be adapted to a company decision on whether to locate production in the home country or a foreign country.

Foreign Direct Investment

A multinational will make a *foreign direct investment* (*FDI*) into an overseas operation to avoid tariffs or other foreign country import barriers, to engage in operational hedging, and so forth. The construction of a new facility is referred to as a *greenfield investment*. However, a cross-border acquisition or merger is often the preferred FDI mode of entry or expansion into foreign markets, where an existing local firm may be acquired by a multinational that wishes to avoid the construction time and other frictions of a greenfield investment.

Other reasons for foreign acquisitions include: consolidating worldwide excess capacity, combining firms in fragmented industries ("roll-ups"), exploiting developed marketing channels, eliminating a competitor, achieving critical mass required for innovative approaches to R&D and production, obtaining an innovation (patent, knowledge, technology), or entering a market to exploit an innovation. In 2007, total worldwide FDI was almost $2 trillion, with roughly half being greenfield investments and the other half being cross-border mergers and acquisitions (M&A). Some additional information on cross-border M&A activity is in the box.

Cross-Border Mergers & Acquisitions

The total volume of cross-border M&A has been growing worldwide, from 23% of the total merger volume in 1998 to 45% in 2007. Recent cross-border M&A activity has mostly been nonconglomerate, instead involving firms in the same industry (*horizontal M&A*) or along the supply/distribution chain (*vertical M&A*). In 1999, about 70% of all global M&As were horizontal. The major industries in which these horizontal combinations occurred were the automobile, pharmaceutical, chemical, food, beverage, tobacco, and more recently telecommunications and utilities. Some of the more well-known ones include Daimler-Benz (Germany)-Chrysler (U.S.); Vodaphone (U.K.)-AirTouch Communications (U.S.); British Petroleum (U.K.)-Amoco and ARCO (U.S.); Alcatel (France)-DSC Communications (U.S.); Deutsche Telecom (Germany)-Voice Stream Wireless (U.S.); and Sony (Japan)-Columbia Pictures (U.S.).

About 90% of cross-border M&A activity in 1999 occurred in developed countries. The great majority of global combinations were between firms in the major western industrial countries. At that time, the foreign targets of U.S. firms (outward U.S. FDI) were primarily located in the United Kingdom, Canada, and Europe. Japan was a relatively minor target of outward U.S. FDI. British firms were the source of the most acquisitions of U.S. firms and in a wide variety of industries. Other acquirers of U.S. firms came from Japan, Netherlands, Canada, Germany, France and other European countries.

The prior trends have been changing. Per *The World Investment Report 2011*, 25% of global M&A activity in 2010 was undertaken in emerging and developing countries. At the same time, investors from these economies are becoming increasingly important players in cross-border M&A markets, which previously were dominated by developed country players.

In a sample of almost 57,000 international M&A deals for the years 1990 to 2007, 80% targeted a non-U.S. firm, while 75% of the acquirers were from outside the United States. The clear majority of cross-border mergers involved private firms as either bidder or target: 96% of the deals involved a private target, 26% involved a private acquirer, and 97% had either private acquirers or targets.

Incremental Cash Flow Application

Often, a capital budgeting analysis involves *incremental* cash flows. Examples include projects to: (a) expand foreign production capacity because of growth in product demand; and (b) replace an operation's old equipment with modern, more efficient equipment.

For an example scenario, we assume that the U.S. multinational Olympic Machine Tools acquired the Austrian company Luna Instruments five years ago. Now, the expected future operating cash flow stream is a level perpetuity of €1m per year. Olympic's managers believe that if the plant equipment is modernized, the production process will be significantly improved. The plant modernization would require a time-0 outlay of €1.2m, and expected operating costs would be lower by €100,000 per year. Thus, the expected operating cash flows in euros would be €1.1m per year instead of €1m. Olympic's managers must decide whether to approve the plant modernization proposal.

Assumptions: (1) From the US dollar perspective, Luna's FX operating exposure to the euro is 1.50 (so the FX exposure to the US dollar is –0.50), and the cost of capital in US dollars is 9%. (2) The euro risk-free rate is 2.39%, $E^*\left(x^{\$/€}\right) = -0.81\%$, $E^*\left(x^{€/\$}\right) = 1.87\%$, and the volatility of percentage changes in the $/€ FX rate is 0.103. (3) The $/€ FX rate is correctly valued at time 0 and expected to be correctly valued in the future. The time-0 spot FX rate is 1.16 $/€, and the forecasted time-1 FX rate is 1.15 $/€. Per equation (4.1), the operation's cost of capital in euros is $(1 + 0.09)[1 + 0.0187] - 1.50(0.103)^2 - 1 = 0.0945$, or 9.45%.

This capital budgeting project involves an incremental expected cash inflow perpetuity in euros of €100,000 per year. The intrinsic value of the expected future incremental cash flows in euros is €100,000/0.0945 =

€1.06m. Since the project does not involve any expected FX windfalls, the NPV in euros may be used for the decision: €1.06m – 1.2m = –€0.14m. The proposal should be rejected.

> *Olympic Machine Tools is considering an alternative plant modernization proposal for Luna Instruments, requiring a time-0 outlay of €800,000 that would reduce expected operating costs by €80,000 per year into perpetuity. Make the same the other assumptions as in the text example. Should Olympic approve the modernization proposal?*
>
> *Answer: The intrinsic value of the incremental expected cash flows is €80,000/0.0945 = €846,561. Since the project does not involve any expected FX windfalls, the NPV in euros may be used for the decision: €846,851 – 800,000 = €46,851. The project should be accepted.*

Change in Political Risk

When you use expected incremental cash flows in an NPV analysis, you are making the implicit assumption that the project's adoption would not change the risk of the operation and thus would not affect the hurdle rate. In many domestic capital budgeting situations, this implicit assumption is acceptable. However, in international capital budgeting applications, it is easy to think of situations where the project will affect the operation's risk and hurdle rate. For example, assume that Olympic Machine Tools Co. is now considering an alternative to the Luna Instruments' plant modernization proposal discussed in the previous text example. Instead, Olympic is now looking at a proposal to produce some components for Luna Instruments in a "cheap labor" country, namely Poland.

A proposal to shift a portion (or all) of production to a different country involves two potential changes to the operation's risk. One potential risk change is related to FX operating exposure. However, in the present scenario, we ignore this possibility for the following reason: Poland has (for now) its own currency, the zloty, not the euro. But in anticipation of eventually joining the Eurozone, the Polish zloty is controlled to "track" the euro closely. So, in this situation, changing the currency denomination of some of the operating costs is not likely to significantly affect Luna's FX operating exposure. We cover the impact of FX operating exposure changes shortly.

The other type of potential risk change is in political risk. In Exhibit 3.2, Poland's political risk premium estimate is 0.65%, whereas Austria's is assumed to be 0 because Austria is a developed country. The operation's new political risk involves two countries. One simple way to handle this situation is to assume that the overall political risk for the operation is driven by the higher political risk country, which is Poland in this case. We apply this approach even though there is plenty of room for judgment here, and some capital budgeting analyses might justify a weighted average approach to the political risk. Also, for simplicity, we assume that the operation's political risk exposure is 1. Since Poland's political risk premium is 65 basis points, the operation's new hurdle rate would be higher by $1[0.0065] = 0.0065$, or 65 basis points. Recall the operation's cost of capital in euros of 9.45%; the operation's new hurdle rate (in euros) would be $9.45\% + 0.65\% = 10.1\%$.

When the capital budgeting proposal involves a change in the hurdle rate, you cannot do an NPV analysis with incremental cash flows. Instead, you need to compare two business alternatives. In the Olympic/Luna case, you need to compare the intrinsic business value after the move with the intrinsic business value before the move and the investment outlay needed to make the move. **To find the NPV of the proposal, you need to find the <u>incremental intrinsic business value,</u> and then subtract the investment outlay.** Luna's intrinsic business value (in euros) before the move is €1m/0.0945 = €10.6m. Assume that the initial outlay at time 0 to shift the component production to Poland is €3m, and that the operating costs would drop by €300,000 per year. So, the new expected operating cash flow stream in euros would be €1.30m a year, perpetually. Luna's new intrinsic business value (in euros) would be €1.30m/0.101 = €12.9m.

The new intrinsic business value of €12.9m is higher than the intrinsic business value before the shift, €10.6m. But the time-0 outlay for the shift is €3m. So, the NPV is negative, because €12.9m – 10.6m – 3m = –€0.7m.

Use the following scenario and redo Olympic's proposal to move component production for the Luna operation to Poland. Assume that the proposal would require an outlay of €1.5m and the future expected operating costs would be reduced by €250,000 per year. Thus, the expected operating cash flows would be €1.25m per year instead of €1m. Assume that the operation's political risk exposure is 1, and that the political risk premium for Poland is 0.65%. Should Olympic approve the proposal?

Answer: Luna's new intrinsic business value (in euros) would be €1.25m/ 0.101 = €12.4m. The new intrinsic business value of €12.4m is higher than the intrinsic business value before the shift, €10.6m. The time-0 outlay for the shift is €1.5m. So, the NPV is positive, because €12.4m – 10.6m – 1.5m = €0.3m. Accept.

Operational Hedging and Beta

A firm that changes its operational hedging strategy changes the FX operating (business) exposure. Changes in operational hedging occur when: (1) a company changes the currency habitat for source materials or other production inputs; or (2) a company changes the currency location of all or part of the production process. Perhaps a U.S. exporter will close a plant in the United States and build or buy a facility in the export market. This production *offshoring* should increase operational hedging and thus reduce the FX operating exposure. Or, a firm could do the reverse, shut down a plant in the overseas market and shift production to the home country. This production *reshoring* would reduce operational hedging, implying a higher (positive) FX operating exposure.

One benefit of lower FX operating exposure is lower operating cash flow volatility and thus lower expected costs of financial distress. Similarly, reducing operational hedging would raise the expected costs of financial distress. So, the capital budgeting analysis of a production relocation decision should, in principle, incorporate the change in the expected financial distress costs, in addition to the change in expected operating cash flows and the net investment outlay required to close production in one country and become operational in the other country.

However, estimating the expected financial distress costs is beyond our scope here.

Instead, we focus on the possibility that a change in FX operating exposure affects an operation's hurdle rate: If the foreign currency has systematic risk, the operational hedging decision may affect the firm's systematic risk and thus the cost of capital. We need to know the impact of a change in the FX exposure to currency C on the operation's beta: In words, the beta change, $\beta_j^H - \beta_i^H$, is equal to the FX exposure change, $\gamma_{Cj}^H - \gamma_{Ci}^H$, times the beta of currency C versus the home currency, β_C^H, as shown in equation (6.1):[1]

Beta and FX Exposure to Currency C

$$\beta_j^H = \beta_i^H + \beta_C^H \left[\gamma_{Cj}^H - \gamma_{Ci}^H \right] \qquad (6.1)$$

To illustrate, assume that if the U.S. exporter Taylor Metals Co. offshores a manufacturing process to the export market in the United Kingdom, the FX operating (business) exposure to the British pound would drop from $\gamma_{\pounds i}^{\$} = 1.50$ to $\gamma_{\pounds j}^{\$} = 0.50$, because of the operational hedging. We want to know the impact of the offshoring on Taylor's business beta. Assume that the currency beta for the British pound versus the US dollar, $\beta_{\pounds}^{\$}$, is 0.20. Let Taylor's initial business beta, $\beta_i^{\$}$, be 0.80. Using equation (6.1), Taylor's new business beta, $\beta_j^{\$}$, is $0.80 + 0.20[0.50 - 1.50] = 0.60$.

By moving production to the United Kingdom, Taylor would lower its business beta to 0.60 (from 0.80), due to the pound's systematic risk, $\beta_{\pounds}^{\$} = 0.20$, and to the lower FX business exposure to the pound. Assume that the GCAPM is the risk–return relationship in US dollars, the US dollar risk-free rate is 3%, and the global risk premium in US dollars is 6%. Taylor's cost of capital is currently $0.03 + 0.80[0.06] = 0.078$, or 7.80%. Taylor's *pro* forma cost of capital, given the decision to offshore the manufacturing process to the United Kingdom, would be lower: $0.03 + 0.60[0.06] = 0.066$, or 6.60%.

Exhibit 6.1 shows some currency beta estimates for various currencies versus the US dollar. The currency beta estimates versus the US dollar may be higher for countries other than those in Exhibit 6.1, because currency betas tend to be higher for emerging countries than developed ones.

Exhibit 6.1 Currency Beta Estimates: Currency C versus US Dollar

Statistical Parameter Estimation Period: 1999–2016	
	$\beta_C^\$$
Eurozone (euro)	0.27
Japan (yen)	−0.03
China (yuan)	0.01
Britain (pound)	0.20
Canada (dollar)	0.37
Australia (dollar)	0.53
Taiwan (dollar)	0.16
Switzerland (franc)	0.17
India (rupee)	0.23
Korea (won)	0.41
Brazil (real)	0.62
Mexico (peso)	0.36
Sweden (krona)	0.41
Hong Kong (dollar)	0.00
Norway (krone)	0.35
Denmark (krone)	0.27
New Zealand (dollar)	0.49
Singapore (dollar)	0.18
South Africa (rand)	0.49
Thailand (baht)	0.18

The U.S. firm Omberg Components Co. makes and exports machine components to Switzerland. Omberg's FX operating exposure to the Swiss franc is 2. Assume that Omberg's operating beta is 1.20, given that the production is in the United States. If Omberg decides to offshore production to Switzerland, the FX operating exposure to the Swiss franc will fall to 1, due to operational hedging. Assume that political risk does not change. (a) If the Swiss franc's currency beta is 0.17 (per Exhibit 6.1), find Omberg's new operating beta if it off-shores production to Switzerland. (b) Assume that the GCAPM is the risk–return trade-off, the risk-free rate in US dollars is 3%, and the global risk premium in US dollars is 6%. Compare the pro forma cost of capital to the current cost of capital.

Answers: (a) Using equation (6.1), Omberg's new operating beta would be 1.20 + 0.17[1 - 2] = 1.03. (b) The new cost of capital would be 0.03 + 1.03[0.06] = 0.0618, or 6.18%, higher than the current cost of capital, 0.03 + 1.20[0.06] = 0.102, or 10.2%.

Of course, it's possible for changes in political risk and FX operating exposure to work in the opposite directions, as the next boxed example illustrates.

The U.S. firm Norton Controls Co. makes and exports electronic controls to Brazil. Norton's FX operating exposure to the Brazilian real is 2.3. Assume that Norton's operating beta in US dollars is 1.82, given that the production is in the United States. If Norton decides to offshore production to Brazil, the FX operating exposure to the real will fall to 1.3, due to operational hedging. Assume that Brazil's political risk premium is 1.15%, per Exhibit 3.2, and that the business has a political risk exposure of 1. (a) If the real's estimated currency beta versus the US dollar is 0.62 (per Exhibit 6.1), find Norton's new operating beta if it offshores production to Brazil. (b) Assume that the GCAPM is the risk–return trade-off, the risk-free rate in US dollars is 3%, and the global risk premium in US dollars is 6%. Compare the current and pro forma hurdle rate in US dollars.

Answers: (a) Using equation (6.1), Norton's new operating beta would be 1.82 + 0.62[1.3 - 2.3] = 1.20. (b) The current cost of capital and hurdle rate in US dollars is 0.03 + 1.82[0.06] = 0.139, or 13.9%. The new hurdle rate in US dollars would be 0.03 + 1.20[0.06] + 1[0.0115] = 0.1135, or 11.35%.

Most currency betas versus the US dollar are positive, like the British pound's beta of 0.20 versus the US dollar. As in the Taylor Metals illustration earlier, a positive currency beta implies that more operational hedging by an exporter results in a lower operating beta and thus a lower cost of capital, and vice versa. However, there is one case of a negative currency beta estimate versus the US dollar in Exhibit 6.1, the Japanese yen. In this case, higher operational hedging, and lower FX operating exposure, imply a *higher* operating beta and cost of capital, and vice versa.

An *importer* may also change FX operating exposure by changing the currency denomination of some operating costs. Say a U.S. firm initially imports raw materials/components from the United Kingdom, with prices fixed in pounds. Assume that the firm's FX operating (business) exposure to the pound is –2, and the business beta is 1.25. If the firm decides to change suppliers, and sources more from the United States, the FX business exposure to the pound will be smaller, say –1. What will happen to the importer's business beta if the currency beta of the pound versus the US dollar is 0.20? Using equation (6.1), the importer's new business beta will be 1.25 + 0.20[–1 – (–2)] = 1.45. So, the importer's business beta is *higher* if the FX operating exposure is smaller.

However, the impact of a change in FX operating (business) exposure is the opposite if the currency beta is negative. Say a U.S. importer sources from Japan. Given the Japanese yen's negative currency beta estimate versus the US dollar, the importer's business beta is lower if the FX operating (business) exposure is smaller, and vice versa. The next boxed example illustrates this impact.

The U.S. firm Denton Machine Co. imports machine components from Japan. Denton's initial FX business exposure to the yen is –1.75 and the business beta is 0.80. If Denton changes the source of some components to the United States, the FX business exposure would be –1.25. (a) If the yen's currency beta estimate is –0.03, find Denton's new business beta if it makes the sourcing change. (b) Assume that the GCAPM is the risk–return trade-off, the risk-free rate in US dollars is 3%, and the global risk premium in US dollars is 6%. Compare the new cost of capital to the current cost of capital.

Answers: (a) Using equation (6.1), Denton's new operating beta is 0.80 – 0.03[–1.25 – (–1.75)] = 0.785. (b) The new cost of capital is 0.03 + 0.785[0.06] = 0.077, or 7.7%. The current cost of capital is 0.03 + 0.80[0.06] = 0.078, or 7.8%. The estimated currency beta is negative, and an importer who reduces a negative FX business exposure has a lower cost of capital.

Increase in Operational Hedging and Business Beta

Currency Beta	Exporter	Importer
Positive	$\beta_B^H \downarrow$	$\beta_B^H \uparrow$
Negative	$\beta_B^H \uparrow$	$\beta_B^H \downarrow$

Different FX Operating Exposures and Project NPV

As we saw earlier, incorporating a hurdle rate change in a capital budgeting analysis requires that we use a slightly different procedure than the traditional one with expected incremental cash flows. The reason is that you only use expected incremental cash flows in the analysis when adopting the project would not cause the hurdle rate to change. If the hurdle rate will change as a direct result of the investment decision, we should use the more general approach of finding the intrinsic business value before and after the investment.

For example, we extend the previous Taylor Metals example. For convenience, we do the NPV analysis in the home currency (US dollars), given the assumption that FX rates are correctly valued to avoid dealing with expected FX windfalls. Assume that from the US dollar perspective, Taylor initially expects operating cash flows of $1,560 per year into perpetuity. So, with Taylor's initial US dollar cost of capital of 7.8%, Taylor's intrinsic business value is initially $1,560/0.078 = $20,000. Assume further that if the production relocation is undertaken, the new expected annual operating cash flow would be $1,500. So, with Taylor's new US dollar cost of capital of 6.60%, the new intrinsic business value would be $1,500/0.0660 = $22,727, an increase in intrinsic business value of $22,727 − 20,000 = $2,727. Assume further that the necessary outlay for the relocation is $1,000. The NPV would be $2,727 − 1,000 = $1,727, and so the relocation decision should be made.

Note that if you ignore the change in the cost of capital, and use the traditional procedure of discounting the incremental expected cash flows using the initial cost of capital, you would mistakenly calculate the NPV to be −$60/0.078 − 1,000 = −$1,669. So, you might mistakenly reject the project because you did not consider the impact of the project on the cost of capital.

Extend the previous boxed example on the U.S. firm Omberg Co. Assume that Omberg initially expects annual operating cash flows of $2.8m into perpetuity and has a cost of capital of 10.2%. If Omberg offshores production to Switzerland, the expected annual operating cash flows would be $3.6m per year and the cost of capital will be 6.18%. Assume that the net investment outlay to complete the offshoring would be $10m. (a) Find the NPV of the offshoring proposal. (b) Should Omberg offshore production to Switzerland? (c) What would be the incorrect NPV of the offshoring proposal if Omberg ignores the cost of capital change?

Answers: (a) NPV = $3.6m/0.0618 − 2.8m/0.102 − 10m = $58.25m − 27.45m − 10m = $20.8m. (b) Accept the relocation proposal because the NPV is positive. (c) The incremental expected perpetual annual operating cash flow is $3.6m − 2.8m = $0.8m. The proposal's incorrect NPV would be $0.8m/0.102 − 10m = $7.84m − 10m = −$2.16m. The negative incorrect NPV would lead to an incorrect decision to reject.

One can adapt the previous scenario to a company's choice between building/buying a plant to produce in the home country versus building/buying a plant to produce in a foreign country. For example, assume that the U.S. firm Thompson Appliance Co. has experienced significant growth in Italian sales, to the point of needing a separate production facility to specifically serve the Italian market. Revenues in euros on Italian sales are expected to be €10m per year forever. If Thompson decides to produce in Italy, the expected annual operating costs in euros will be 75% of expected revenues, and the investment outlay for the plant will be €20m. From the US dollar perspective, the FX operating exposure to the euro would be 1.20 (so the FX exposure to the US dollar is −0.20), and the operating beta would be 1. Using the GCAPM with a US dollar risk-free rate of 3% and US dollar global risk premium of 6%, the operation's cost of capital in US dollars would be 9%.

If Thompson instead decides to produce in the United States, the expected annual operating costs (including shipping and other export costs) will be 80% of expected revenues (after conversion to US dollars), and the investment outlay for the plant will be $15m. A "what if" analysis suggests that the FX operating exposure to the euro would be 4.70. Other assumptions: (1) $E^*\left(x^{\$/€}\right) = -0.81\%$, $E^*\left(x^{€/\$}\right) = 1.87\%$, and the volatility of percentage changes in the $\$/€$ FX rate is 0.103. (2) The $\$/€$ FX rate is correctly valued at time 0 and expected to be correctly valued in the future. The time-0 spot FX rate is 1.16 $\$/€$, and the forecasted time-1 FX rate is 1.15 $\$/€$.

If Thompson decides to produce in Italy, the operation's cost of capital in euros, per equation (4.1), is $(1 + 0.09)[1 + 0.0187] - 1.20(0.103)^2 - 1 = 0.0977$, or 9.77%. The NPV in euros for the Italian plant option is €2.5m/0.0977 – 20m = €5.59m, which is equivalent to an NPV in US dollars of (€5.59m)(1.16 $\$/€$) = $6.48m.

If Thompson decides to produce in the United States, the expected time-1 revenue in US dollars, per equation (4.3), is €10m(1.15 $\$/€$)[1 – (–0.20)(0.103)^2] = $11.52m, and the expected operating cash flow in US dollars is 0.20($11.52m) = $2.3m. The euro's currency beta versus the US dollar is 0.27 per Exhibit 6.1; applying equation (6.1) to estimate the operation's beta with U.S. production yields: 1 + 0.27[4.70 – 1.20] = 1.945. Therefore, the operation's new cost of capital in US dollars would be 0.03 + 1.945[0.06] = 0.1467, or 14.67%. Assuming a perpetual expected cash flow in US dollars of $2.3m, the NPV in US dollars for the U.S. plant option is $2.3m/0.1467 – 15m = $0.68m. The Italian plant option has a higher NPV in US dollars, $6.48m versus $0.68m.

The U.S. firm Thompson Appliance Co. has experienced significant growth in Norwegian sales, to the point of needing a separate production facility to serve the Norwegian market. Revenues in Norwegian kroner are expected to be Nk100m per year forever. If Thompson decides to produce in Norway, the expected annual operating costs in kroner will be 75% of expected revenues, and the investment outlay for the plant will be Nk200m. From the US dollar perspective, the FX operating exposure to the krone would be 1.20 *(so the FX exposure to the US dollar = -0.20), and the operating beta would be 1. Using the GCAPM with a US dollar risk-free rate of 3% and US dollar global risk premium of 6%, the operation's cost of capital in US dollars would be 9%. If Thompson decides to produce in the United States, the expected annual operating costs (including shipping and other export costs) will be 80% of expected revenues (in US dollars), the investment outlay for the plant will be $15 m, and a "what if" analysis suggests that the FX operating exposure to the krone would be 4.7. Other assumptions: (1) $E^*\left(x^{\$/Nk}\right) = 0$, $E^*\left(x^{Nk/\$}\right) = 1.28\%$, the volatility of percentage changes in the $/Nk FX rate is 0.116, and the krone's currency beta versus the US dollar is 0.35, per Exhibit 6.1. (2) The $/Nk FX rate is correctly valued at time 0 and expected to be correctly valued in the future. In direct terms from the US dollar point of view, the time-0 spot FX rate is 0.12 $/Nk, and the forecasted time-1 FX rate is the same, 0.12 $/Nk. (a) Find the NPV of the Norwegian production option in kroner. (b) Find the NPV of the U.S. production operation in US dollars.*

Answers: (a) Producing in Norway, the operation's cost of capital in kroner, per equation (4.1) is $(1 + 0.09)[1 + 0.0128] - 1.20(0.116)^2 - 1 = 0.0878$, or 8.78%. The NPV in kroner for the Norwegian plant option is Nk25m/0.0878 - 200m = Nk84.7m, which is equivalent to an NPV in US dollars of (Nk84.7m)(0.12 $/Nk) = $10.2m. (b) With U.S. production, the expected time-1 revenue in US dollars, per equation (4.3), is Nk100m(0.12 $/Nk)[1 - (-0.20)(0.116)^2] = $12m, and the expected operating cash flow in US dollars is 0.20($12m) = $2.4m. Apply equation (6.1) to estimate the operation's beta with U.S. production: $1 + 0.35[4.70 - 1.20] = 2.25$. Therefore, the cost of capital would be $0.03 + 2.25[0.06] = 0.165$, or 16.5%. Assuming a perpetual expected cash flow in US dollars of $2.4m, the NPV in US dollars for the U.S. plant option is $2.4m/0.165 - 15m = -$0.45m. The Norwegian plant option has a higher NPV in US dollars, $10.2m versus -$0.45m. One reason why the Norwegian plant option is better is that the U.S. plant option's cost of capital is higher because of the higher FX operating exposure.

Operational Hedging and the ICAPM

A change in a firm's FX operating exposure to a specific currency may sometimes also result in a material change in the firm's FX business exposure to the ICAPM **foreign currency index**, γ_{Bi}^{H}. We ignore this possibility for the US dollar perspective, because γ_{Bi}^{H} does not have much impact on the cost of capital estimate in US dollars. For home currencies where we want to apply the ICAPM to estimate the cost of capital, we need to consider the impact of an FX operating (business) exposure change on γ_{Bi}^{H}.

The impact on γ_{Bi}^{H} depends on the exposure-currency's weight in the home currency's foreign currency index. Equation (6.2) shows the general formula for the change in FX exposure to the (wealth-weighted) ICAPM foreign currency index for a given change in a firm's FX exposure to currency C in the index.

FX Exposure to ICAPM FX Index

$$\gamma_j^H = \gamma_i^H + \left[w_C / \left(1 - w_H \right) \right] \left[\gamma_{Cj}^H - \gamma_{Ci}^H \right] \qquad (6.2)$$

For example, from the euro perspective, assume that the US dollar's weight in the ICAPM foreign currency index, $w_\$ / (1 - w_\euro)$, is 47.6% (per Chapter 2). Consider a Eurozone exporter to the United States that has an initial FX business exposure to the US dollar, $\gamma_{B\$}^{\euro}$, of 2, and an initial FX business exposure to the ICAPM foreign currency index, $\gamma_{B}^{\euro}$, of 0.80. The company relocates some production to the United States, which lowers the FX operating (business) exposure to the US dollar to 1.40. Per equation (6.2), the new $\gamma_{B}^{\euro}$ will be 0.80 + 0.476[1.40 - 2] = 0.51.

Next, we use equation (6.1) and the US dollar's currency beta versus the euro, 0.155 (per Exhibit 4.1), to find the company's new business beta if the initial business beta is 0.90: $\beta_{Bj}^{\euro} = 0.90 + 0.155[1.40 - 2] = 0.807$.

Finally, we compare the new cost of capital to the initial cost of capital using the ICAPM in equation (2.2) from the euro perspective, with inputs from Exhibit 2.2: $GRP_1^{\euro} = 5.54\%$ and $XRP_1^{\euro} = -0.92\%$. Also, assume that the euro risk-free rate is 2.5%. The initial cost of capital is 0.025 + 0.90[0.0554] + 0.80[-0.0092] = 0.0675, or 6.75%. The new cost of capital is 0.025 + 0.807[0.0554] + 0.51[-0.0092] = 0.065, or 6.50%.

The British firm London Tools Ltd. exports machine components to United States buyers. London Tools' initial FX operating (business) exposure to the US dollar is 1.75, the business beta is 1.20, and the FX business exposure to the ICAPM foreign currency index is 0.90. London Tools is considering moving some of the latter stages of manufacturing to the United States for operational hedging, and so would lower the FX business exposure to the US dollar to 1.25. (a) Find the proportion of the US dollar in the ICAPM foreign currency index portfolio from the British pound perspective. Hint: See Exhibit 5.4. (b) Find London Tools' new FX business exposure to the foreign currency index. (c) The US dollar's currency beta versus the pound is 0.087, per Exhibit 6.3. Find London's new business beta. (d) Use the ICAPM risk-return expression in equation (2.2) from the British pound perspective; assume that the pound risk-free rate is 3.50%; and use inputs from the British pound perspective from Exhibit 5.4. Compare the new cost of capital to the current cost of capital.

Answers: (a) $w_\$ / (1 - w_£) = 0.379/(1 - 0.066) = 0.406$. (b) Per equation (6.2), the new FX business exposure to the ICAPM foreign currency index is $0.90 + 0.406[1.25 - 1.75] = 0.70$. (c) Per equation (6.1), the new business beta is $1.20 + 0.087[1.25 - 1.75] = 1.16$. (d) The initial cost of capital is $0.035 + 1.20[0.0559] + 0.90[-0.0071] = 0.0957$, or 9.57%. The new cost of capital is equal to $0.035 + 1.16[0.0559] + 0.70[-0.0071] = 0.0949$, or 9.49%.

Summary Action Points

- A capital budgeting proposal to relocate production to a different country should take into consideration the impact of the move on political risk, FX risk, and the hurdle rate.
- If the currency beta of the foreign currency is not zero, a firm's business beta will change if the FX business exposure changes. The resulting change in the firm's cost of capital needs to be considered as part of the financial evaluation of the capital budgeting proposals that change FX operating exposure.

- When using the ICAPM to estimate cost of capital, one should also investigate how an FX business exposure change will affect the FX business exposure to the foreign currency index.

Glossary

Greenfield Investment: The construction of a new plant or facility.

Horizontal M&A: Merger or acquisition involving firms in the same industry.

Offshoring: A change of production location by an exporter from the home country to the export market.

Reshoring: A change of production location by an exporter from the export market to the home country.

Vertical M&A: Merger or acquisition involving firms of a supply or distribution chain.

Problems

1. The U.S. firm Renwick Co. has a U.K. subsidiary in that is expected to generate £100,000 in operating cash flow each year into perpetuity. A "what if" analysis shows that the subsidiary's FX operating exposure to the British pound is 0.70. The cost of capital in US dollars for the subsidiary is 8%. Renwick is evaluating a plant modernization proposal by the U.K. subsidiary that would require an outlay of £100,000. At the same time, the expected operating costs would be reduced by £10,000 per year. Thus, the new expected operating cash flows in British pounds would be £110,000 per year instead of £100,000. Assume: (1) the time-0 spot FX rate is 1.30 $/£; (2) the expected rate of change in the FX price of the British pound versus the US dollar is 0.42% per year; and (3) the volatility of percentage changes in the British pound versus the US dollar is 0.085. Renwick's management believes that the FX rates are always correctly valued. Find the NPV of the

modernization proposal in US dollars. Should Renwick approve the modernization proposal?

2. The U.S. firm Robichek & Myers Co. has a subsidiary in Brazil that makes machine tools for sale locally in Brazil. All parts, raw materials, and labor are sourced locally in Brazil. R&M has become worried about the impact of political risk on the availability of some parts and raw materials, and proposes to replace some of the Brazilian suppliers with U.S. suppliers. The managers estimate that the operation's political risk exposure would drop from 1.50 to 1, but that the FX operating exposure to the Brazilian real would rise from 1.3 to 2.0, due to less operational hedging. Assume that the operating beta in US dollars is presently 1.20, given that all suppliers are in Brazil. Assume that Brazil's political risk premium is 1.15%, per Exhibit 3.2. (a) If the real's estimated currency beta versus the US dollar is 0.62 (per Exhibit 6.1), find R&M's new operating beta with the new supply plan. (b) Assume that the GCAPM is the risk–return trade-off, the risk-free rate in US dollars is 3%, and the global risk premium in US dollars is 6%. Compare the current and pro forma hurdle rate in US dollars. (c) If the new supply plan requires no time-0 investment outlay, and would not change the operation's expected operating cash flows in US dollars, should the plan be accepted or rejected?

3. Blackstone Co. is a U.S. firm that sources raw materials and parts from the United States. Blackstone's business beta is 0.80. Blackstone is considering a proposal to change a supplier to a British firm whose prices are fixed in British pounds. Blackstone's FX operating (business) exposure to the pound would change from 0 to -1.50. What will happen to Blackstone's business beta if the currency beta of the pound versus the US dollar is 0.20?

Answers to Problems

1. Since there are no expected FX windfalls, the foreign currency approach is easy. The tricky part is to use equation (5.2) to approximate the equilibrium expected rate of change in the US dollar versus the British pound, which is $-0.0042 + (0.085)^2 = 0.003$, or 0.30%.

Using equation (4.1), the cost of capital in British pounds is (1.08) [1 + 0.003] – 0.70(0.085)^2 – 1 = 0.078, or 7.8%. The NPV in British pounds is £10,000/0.078 – £100,000 = £28,205, which is equivalent to £28,205(1.30 $/£) = $36,667, the NPV in US dollars. Since the NPV > 0, accept the proposal.

2. (a) Using equation (6.1), the new operating beta would be 1.20 + 0.62[2.0 – 1.3] = 1.63. (b) In US dollars, the current cost of capital is 0.03 + 1.20[0.06] = 0.102, or 10.2%, and current hurdle rate is 10.2% + 1.50[1.15%] = 11.9%. The new hurdle rate in US dollars would be 0.03 + 1.63[0.06] + 1[0.0115] = 0.139, or 13.9%. (c) Reject, because the hurdle rate is higher with the new plan, so the intrinsic business value will be lower if the expected operating cash flow stream does not change.

3. Using equation (6.1), Blackstone's new business beta will be equal to 0.80 + 0.20[–1.50 – 0] = 0.50. So, the business beta is *lower* even though there is more FX operating exposure.

Discussion Questions

1. If the currency beta is positive, what is the impact on the cost of capital of offshoring production to the export market country? Explain.
2. What is the impact on the cost of capital of an importer that reduces sourcing from an exporting country, if that country's currency beta is positive? Explain.
3. What is the impact on the cost of capital of an importer that reduces sourcing from an exporting country, if that country's currency beta is negative? Explain.

CASE STUDY

New Plant for Houston Marine Electronics

International Cost of Capital and Capital Budgeting

Sitting behind his desk, Ben Nunnally told Reid Click, "We need to do an analysis of HME's request for more plant capacity." Their meeting was taking place in May 2013 in Nunnally's office at Adventure & Recreation Technologies, Inc. (ART), in Boise, Idaho. Nunnally had been ART's Chief Financial Officer (CFO) and Treasurer since before the company went public in the 1980s, and Click had been with the company for five years as an Assistant Treasurer.

ART is the parent company of three businesses: (1) Divemaster (scuba equipment); (2) Houston Marine Electronics (HME) (sonar equipment); and (3) Watercraft (canoes and kayaks). ART's strategy across its three business segments is to use sophisticated research and cutting-edge technology to create the world's best-known brands of outdoor recreational products.

The previous week, HME's Chief Executive Officer (CEO), William "King" Kennedy, and CFO, Stafford Johnson, traveled to the ART headquarters in Boise and made a presentation to Nunnally and Click. The presentation outlined the increasing orders from Australia for HME's sonar equipment and the shortage of production capacity to keep up with the growing demand. HME's three plants in the United States were already producing at full capacity. HME had recently signed a two-year contract with the Australian boat builder Gold Coast Ships, and HME's operations managers were already straining to stay on production schedule. In the meantime, HME's head of sales, Steve Magee, reported that many other Australian and New Zealand boat builders had expressed a keen interest in putting HME's sonar equipment in their boats. Simply put, Kennedy and Johnson were letting the ART corporate officers know that HME needed additional production capacity dedicated to the Australian market. The HME executives also knew that ART had accumulated about $60 million in cash, some of which could be used for the capital expenditure.

Nunnally continued talking to Click, "Magee says that HME's sonar units will penetrate the Australian market quickly. He strongly suggests stabilizing the product price in Australian dollars, which means we'll be looking at some FX risk because of uncertainty in the future $/A$ FX rate. With the pricing strategy Magee projects, we should get **Australian revenues of A$10 million per year**."

Nunnally continued, "It seems clear that HME needs additional plant capacity for the Australian business. I expect that the numbers will support the strategy of overseas sales expansion as a sound business move. Still, I am asking you to prepare a formal capital budgeting analysis. One thing on the table is the plant location. I want you to consider two location options: (a) Australia; and (b) the United States."

Click returned to his office and immediately began to think about the project. He understood the inputs needed for a net present value (NPV) analysis are: (a) the hurdle rate, based on the cost of capital; (b) an estimate of the expected operating cash flow stream; and (c) the investment outlay. Each of these inputs depended on the location of the plant. The international nature of the capital budgeting problem required that he also do some FX rate research.

Click had recently helped estimate ART's overall cost of capital, successfully arguing that the modern integration of global financial markets implies that ART's equity beta should be estimated relative to a global equity index (measured in US dollars) and not a U.S. stock index. Using historical monthly equity rates of return for 2007 to 2011, Click had estimated **ART's global equity beta is 1.28**, compared to a local equity beta of 1.43 relative to the S&P 500 index. ART's relatively high beta estimates are consistent with the notion that its high-end recreational products are "luxuries" that have a relatively high income elasticity of demand. (At the other end of the spectrum, companies that sell "necessities" such as food and basic apparel, with low income elasticity of demand, tend to have low betas, all else the same.)

During 2007 to 2011, ART had gradually paid off all its $60 million in debt and accumulated $60 million in cash and marketable securities. Click reasoned that because ART's average net debt was 0 during the 2007 to 2011 period, he was comfortable with an estimate of **1.28 for ART's overall operating beta.** (Q1)

Australian Production Option

Click decided to first estimate the project's NPV assuming production in Australia. Using the typical HME experience of operating costs of 75% of revenues, Click estimated **annual operating costs of A$7.5 million.** Therefore, he decided to base the NPV analysis on a **perpetual expected operating cash flow stream of A$2.5 million per year.**

Click knew that he could not just apply ART's overall operating beta estimate of 1.28 for an operation in Australia. He needed a cost of capital, and thus an operating beta, specific to the operation. For the Australian production option, Click decided to use the Lessard country beta method, with ART as the home country proxy firm. With **country beta estimates (in US dollars, versus the global equity index) of 1.16 for Australia and 0.94 for the United States,** Click estimated a **project operating beta of 1.58, given production in Australia.** (Q2)

To find a cost of capital estimate in US dollars, Click used the global CAPM (GCAPM), assuming: (a) a global risk premium of 6%; and (b) a US dollar risk-free rate of 3%, based on the 30-year Treasury yield. He decided not to adjust for political risk because of Australia's developed country status. Click estimated the operation's **cost of capital (and hurdle rate) is 12.5%, in US dollars, for the Australian production option.** (Q3)

Click knew that he needed to convert the 12.5% cost of capital estimate from US dollars to Australian dollars. For the conversion, he would need estimates of (1) the project's FX business exposure to the Australian dollar, from the US dollar perspective; (2) the volatility of $/A$ FX rate changes; and (3) the expected rate of intrinsic FX change of the US dollar versus the Australian dollar.

(1) Using a "what if" analysis, he estimated an **FX business exposure to the Australian dollar of 1.40,** inclusive of an economic "demand

effect" of changes in the $/A$ FX rate. (2) He found an estimate of **12.7% for the volatility of the $/A$ FX rate**. (3) Finally, based on a currency risk premium estimate of –1.38% for the US dollar versus the Australian dollar, an **Australian dollar risk-free rate of 6.84% and a US dollar risk-free rate of 3%**, Click estimated an **expected rate of intrinsic FX change of 2.46% per year for the US dollar versus the Australian dollar**. (Q4)

Putting all the inputs together, Click estimated a project **hurdle rate in Australian dollars of 13%**. (Q5)

A commercial real estate contact in Australia suggested to Click that a plant facility to make the sonar devices in Australia would likely require an outlay of A$18 million. Based on the assumption of a perpetual annual expected operating cash flow of A$2.5 million, Click estimated a **project NPV in Australian dollars of A$1.23 million**. (Q6)

Although the project's NPV in Australian dollars was positive, Click believed that the more important NPV in cross-border valuation is from the perspective of ART's home currency, the US dollar. At the time, the **spot FX rate was 1.08 $/A$**. Based on research supplied by ART's bank and other sources, Click estimated the **Australian dollar was overvalued by 8% versus the US dollar**, implying an **intrinsic time-0 spot FX rate of 1 $/A$**.

Click assumed that Australian dollar would likely give up the 8% overvaluation gradually over the next four years and be correctly valued versus the US dollar from that time forward. He estimated an **expected intrinsic rate of FX change of the Australian dollar versus the US dollar of –0.85% per year**. At this rate of intrinsic FX change, the **expected future intrinsic spot FX rates would be 0.992 $/A$ at time 1, 0.983 $/A$ at time 2, 0.975 $/A$ at time 3, and 0.966 $/A$ at time 4**. (Q7)

To estimate FX forecasts consistent with the actual spot FX rate gradually dropping from 1.08 $/A$ at time 0 to 0.966 $/A$ as of time 4, Click's **actual spot FX rate forecasts were 1.05 $/A$ at time 1, 1.02 $/A$ at time 2, 0.99 $/A$ at time 3, and 0.996 $/A$ at time 4**.

Click realized that if he converted the expected Australian dollar operating cash flow stream to US dollars using the actual spot FX rate forecasts, the result would be expected cash flows in US dollars that contained an FX windfall gain because of the Australian dollar's overvaluation versus the US dollar, in addition to the business cash flows. He knew that at the intrinsic spot FX rate, the present value of the business cash flows had to be equivalent across the two currency perspectives. He would find the present value of the FX windfall portion of the cash flows separately, using as the discount rate the **equilibrium required rate of return on a risk-free Australian dollar deposit, 5.99%. The present value of the expected FX windfalls in the future cash flows is $0.255m.** (Q8)

Given the time-0 outlay of A$18m for the Australian plant, Click estimated an **NPV in US dollars of $50,000.** Click saw that the NPV in US dollars was relatively small, compared to the one in Australian dollars, because of the need to convert US dollars to Australian dollars for the plant outlay at time 0, at a spot FX rate that represented an overvalued Australian dollar versus the US dollar. (Q9)

United States Production Option

Click next wanted to find an NPV estimate in US dollars if production were in the United States. He understood that with U.S. production instead of Australian, there would be "some good news and some bad news."

The "good news" had two parts: (1) the FX windfall would be higher, because only the revenues would be converted at the future FX rates that are projected to reflect an overvalued Australian dollar versus the US dollar; and (2) the US dollar outlay for the plant facility would not have to be converted to Australian dollars at the time-0 spot FX rate that reflected an overvalued Australian dollar versus the US dollar.

The "bad news" was that HME would have no operational hedging of the FX risk of the Australian revenue stream, and so the FX operating exposure to the Australian dollar would be higher. Given the **Australian dollar's estimated currency beta versus the US dollar of 0.53**, a higher FX operating exposure implies a higher operating beta and thus a higher cost of capital.

Click understood that regardless of the plant location, some operating costs will be in Australia, in Australian dollars, including costs of selling, distribution, installation, service, and so forth. He estimated these costs to be 10% of revenues. Therefore, he expected an annual net amount in

Australian dollars of **A\$9m**. When Click converted this stream to US dollars, he found that an annual amount \$9m was close enough to use in the analysis. (Q10)

The rest of the operating costs would be incurred in the United States, in US dollars. Of course, there would be some shipping and other exporting expenses, but he decided to use the standard estimate for total operating costs as 75% of revenues, which implied U.S. operating costs of 65% of revenues.

Click next estimated a project cost of capital in US dollars, assuming manufacturing in the United States. Click estimated an **operating beta of 3.17 in US dollars, given U.S. production**, which implied a **cost of capital (and hurdle rate) of 22%, in US dollars**. (Q11)

Click's analysis showed that for an outlay of \$18m for the U.S. facility, **the U.S. production option's NPV is -\$5.7m**. Click's analysis thus showed that the "bad news" (about the lower operational hedging) outweighed the "good news" (about the higher FX windfalls), and the Australian production option was clearly better than the U.S one. (Q12)

Click was prepared to recommend the Australian production option, based on the higher NPV in US dollars. But he leaned back in his chair and began to think about other considerations in the decision. (Q13)

Questions

1. Explain why ART's operating beta estimate is the same as its equity beta estimate.
2. Show how Click estimated a project operating beta of 1.58.
3. Show how Click estimated a project cost of capital of 12.5% (in US dollars), given production in Australia.
4. Show how Click estimated 2.46% for the expected rate of intrinsic FX change of the US dollar versus the Australian dollar.
5. Show how Click estimated 13% for the project's cost of capital in Australian dollars. Hint: you need to use the cost of capital conversion equation:

$$1 + k_i^{A\$} = \left(1 + k_i^{\$}\right)\left[1 + E^*(x^{A\$/\$})\right] - \gamma_{iA\$}^{\$}\left(\sigma_{A\$}^{\$}\right)^2$$

6. Show how Click got the Australian dollar NPV estimate of A$1.23m.

7. Confirm Click's estimate of -0.85% using $\sigma_{A\$}^{\$} = 0.127$ and the equation $E(x^{\$/A\$}) = -E(x^{A\$/\$}) + (\sigma_{A\$}^{\$})^2$. Confirm the estimates for the expected intrinsic FX rates.

8. Show how Click estimated the equilibrium required rate of return on a risk-free Australian dollar deposit, 5.99%, and the present value of the expected FX windfalls in the future cash flows, $0.255m.

9. Show how Click found the US dollar NPV estimate of $50,000.

10. The actual expected time-1 amount in US dollars is $8.98m. Show how to get this amount.

11. Show how Click got the cost of capital estimate of 22%, given production in the United States. You will need to find the project's "new" operating beta, given U.S. production, 3.17. The "new" estimate of FX operating exposure to the Australian dollar is 4.40. Use the idea that the difference in operating beta is equal to the currency beta times the difference in FX operating exposure.

12. Show how Click estimated the US dollar NPV of -$5.7m.

13. What are some other considerations in the choice between Australian and U.S. production?

Notes

Chapter 1

1. These results are in Brotherson et al. (2013), Da, Guo, and Jagannathan (2012), and Welch (2009).
2. See Brotherson et al. (2013).
3. See Luehrman and Heilprin (2009); Welch (2009); Donaldson, Kamstra, and Kramer (2010); and Fernandez, Aguirreamalloa, and Avendaño (2012).
4. The distinction between the global market index and the world market index is noted in Stulz (1995b).
5. See Krapl and O'Brien (2016).
6. See Bryan (2007) and Maldonado and Saunders (1983).
7. See Baruch, Karolyi, and Lemmon (2007). For trends in cross-listing, see Halling et al. (2008).
8. For dual-listed shares, see Froot and Dabora (1999) and de Jong, Rosenthal, and Van Dijk (2009). For Chinese A-shares and B-shares, see Mei, Scheinkman, and Xiong (2009). Also, see Arquette, Brown, and Burdekin (2008).

Chapter 2

1. FX exposure is explained in detail in O'Brien (2017).
2. The currency index could also be constructed to contain currency H, so that the index's composition is the same for every currency, in which case there is no w_H term when finding XRP_1^H. However, it is somewhat confusing to think about an index's change against currency H when the index also contains currency H, so we restrict the currency index to consist of only foreign currencies from the perspective of currency H and include the adjustment for w_H.
3. $\beta_i^{\prime C} = [cov(R_i^C, R_X^C)\sigma_X^2 - cov(R_i^C, R_G^C)cov(R_G^C, R_X^C)]/[\sigma_G^2\sigma_X^2 - cov(R_G^C, R_X^C)^2]$,

    and

    $\gamma_i^{\prime C} = [cov(R_i^C, R_X^C)\sigma_G^2 - cov(R_i^C, R_G^C)cov(R_G^C, R_X^C)]/[\sigma_G^2\sigma_X^2 - cov(R_G^C, R_X^C)^2]$
4. Stulz (1995a, 1995b) also "anchored" international GRP estimates to the local U.S. market risk premium estimate.
5. The two-factor ICAPM version represented by equations (2.1) and (2.2) is based on a simplification by Ross and Walsh (1983) of the "Solnik (1974) –

Sercu (1980) special case" of the general ICAPM (Adler and Dumas 1983). Ignoring currency superscripts, the fundamental risk-pricing relation of the Solnik-Sercu model, adapted from equation (2.9) in Dumas (1994), is: $RP_i = qcov(R_i,R_G) + \Sigma_{C \neq H} \, q(1/q_C - 1)cov(R_i,x^{H/C})(W_C/W)$, where RP_i is asset i's required risk premium, equal to asset's required rate of return, k_i, minus the nominal currency-H risk-free rate; R_i is asset i's return, consisting of the asset's local currency return and the change in the value of the asset's currency versus currency H; R_G is the return in currency H on the *unhedged* global market index; $x^{H/C}$ is the percentage change in currency C versus currency H; W_C is the wealth of the economy using currency C; q_C is the average degree of risk aversion of investors in the economy using currency C; W is total global wealth; and q is the global (harmonic mean) degree of risk aversion (over all economies, including H): $1/q = [\Sigma_C(W_C/q_C)]/W$.

The currency risk factors may be aggregated into a portfolio, but with generally unobservable weights (Solnik 1997). However, assuming the same average degree of risk aversion across economies, $q_C = \Theta$ for all C (including H) implies that q in the risk-pricing equation also takes the value Θ, the global market price of risk. In this case, the weights in the currency portfolio are W_C/W (Ross and Walsh 1983).

To make the currency weights into foreign currency portfolio weights that sum to 1, let $w_C = W_C/(W - W_H)$, the percentage of economy C's wealth of the world wealth outside of economy H. Then $W_C/W = (1 - w_H)$ W_C. The resulting simplified risk-pricing model in only two factors is: $E(R_i) = \Theta cov(R_i,R_G) + (1 - \Theta)(1 - w_H)cov(R_i,R_X)$, where R_X is the return in currency H on a wealth-weighted portfolio of all other currencies, $\Sigma_{C \neq H} w_C x^{H/C}$.

Equation (2.2) follows by noting that and $cov(R_i,R_G) = \beta_i \sigma_G^2$ and using $cov(R_i,R_X) = \gamma_i \sigma_X^2$, the definitions of the components of the global risk premium and foreign currency index risk premium. Equation (2.1) requires aggregating the simplified risk-pricing model twice, first over all assets to get the global market risk premium, and then over all currencies to get the foreign currency index risk premium. Equation (2.1) follows by solving the two aggregate equations simultaneously for Θ and $(1 - \Theta)$.

The equal risk aversion assumption may seem restrictive, but why would the average degree of risk aversion in the Eurozone be much different than that in the United States, or the United Kingdom, and so forth? It seems likely that China's degree of risk aversion is relatively low, but this is inconsequential because the yuan does not have much volatility versus the US dollar. Moreover, the assumption is not nearly as unrealistic as the standard "homogeneous expectations" assumption of all CAPMs, that all investors have the same estimates of the expected rate of return and risk parameters for all assets. In his GCAPM analysis, Stulz (1995b, p. 12) seems to have no problem with the assumption that "investors are the same across countries in their preferences."

6. See Krapl and O'Brien (2016).
7. Sercu (1980) and Ross and Walsh (1983) show that if the GCAPM holds from one currency perspective, the consistent risk-return model from any other currency perspective must be a two-factor model, with the FX rate between the currencies being the second factor.

Chapter 3

1. See "Bank of America Roundtable on Evaluating and Financing Foreign Direct Investment" (1996).
2. This point is made in Pettit, Ferguson, and Gluck (1999) and Block (2003). Also, see Krüger, Landier, and Thesmar (2015).
3. Weston (1973) pioneered the idea using the traditional CAPM for finding an operation-specific cost of capital.
4. Desai (2006) uses this formula in his Harvard case on the cost of capital for AES Corporation.
5. Other country beta estimates are in Perold (2004).
6. See Lessard (1996). The only difference is that the betas in the original Lessard analysis are relative to the local market index, whereas the betas in equation (3.2) are relative to the global market index.
7. For further details, see Bekaert et al. (2016).
8. Abuaf (2015) advocates Φ_i = 0.35, 0.70, and 1 for the low, medium, and high political risk exposure categories, but he also uses the full sovereign CDS yield for the political risk premium. Basically, the Abuaf (2015) model makes the simplifying assumption that all countries have the same ratio of political risk premium to sovereign risk premium of about 0.70.
9. Damodaran (2003) pioneered the idea of this type of exposure, but called the factor "country risk" instead of political risk, and used the exposure notation λ_i instead of Φ_i. Technically, country risk includes the equity market's volatility, and so political risk is an even smaller portion of country risk than of sovereign risk, for example, Click and Wiener (2010).
10. Equation (3.4) adapts ideas from diverse places in the literature, such as Zenner and Akaydin (2002), Godfrey and Espinosa (1996), Harvey (2000), and Damodaran, op. cit. Also, see Bekaert, et al., op. cit. for insights and a review of this literature.

Chapter 4

1. To derive equation (4.1), start with equation (1.1a): $1 + R_i^{\text{€}} = (1 + R_i^{\$})$ $(1 + x^{\text{€}/\$})$. Multiply out the right-hand side to get $1 + R_i^{\text{€}} = 1 + R_i^{\$} + x^{\text{€}/\$}$ $+ R_i^{\$} x^{\text{€}/\$}$. Take expectations to get $1 + E(R_i^{\text{€}}) = 1 + E(R_i^{\$}) + E(x^{\text{€}/\$})$ $+ E(R_i^{\$} x^{\text{€}/\$})$. The term $E(R_i^{\$} x^{\text{€}/\$})$ is equal to $E(R_i^{\$}) \bullet E(x^{\text{€}/\$}) + cov(R_i^{\$},$ $x^{\text{€}/\$})$, so we substitute and get $1 + E(R_i^{\text{€}}) = 1 + E(R_i^{\$}) + E(x^{\text{€}/\$})$ $+ E(R_i^{\$}) \bullet E(x^{\text{€}/\$}) + cov(R_i^{\$}, x^{\text{€}/\$})$, which simplifies to $1 + E(R_i^{\text{€}}) =$ $\left[1 + E(R_i^{\$})\right]\left[1 + E(x^{\text{€}/\$})\right] + cov(R_i^{\$}, x^{\text{€}/\$})$. Because $cov(R_i^{\$}, x^{\text{€}/\$}) = -cov(R_i^{\$},$ $x^{\$/\text{€}}) = -\gamma_{i\text{€}}^{\$}(\sigma_{\text{€}}^{\$})^2$, we get that $1 + E(R_i^{\text{€}}) = \left[1 + E(R_i^{\$})\right]\left[1 + E(x^{\text{€}/\$})\right]$ $- \gamma_{i\text{€}}^{\$}(\sigma_{\text{€}}^{\$})^2$. Expressing the expectations as *equilibrium* concepts, we get the cost of capital conversion formula in equation (4.1), where $\$ = H$ and $\text{€} = C$.

2. To derive equation (4.3), start with the definition: $O_N^{\$} = O_N^{\text{€}} \bullet X_N^{\$/\text{€}}$. Thus, $E(O_N^{\$}) = E(O_N^{\text{€}}) \bullet E(X_N^{\$/\text{€}}) + cov(O_N^{\text{€}}, X_N^{\$/\text{€}})$. Rewrite the covariance term: $E(O_N^{\text{€}}) \bullet E(X_N^{\$/\text{€}}) cov(O_N^{\text{€}}/E(O_N^{\text{€}}) - 1, X_N^{\$/\text{€}}/E(X_N^{\$/\text{€}}) - 1)$, where the new covariance term is the covariance between the percentage deviation of $O_N^{\text{€}}$ from $E(O_N^{\text{€}})$, and the percentage deviation of $X_N^{\$/\text{€}}$ from $E(X_N^{\$/\text{€}})$. Using the approximation, $X_N^{\$/\text{€}}/E(X_N^{\$/\text{€}}) - 1 = -(X_N^{\text{€}/\$}/E(X_N^{\text{€}/\$}) - 1)$, the covariance term becomes $cov[O_N^{\text{€}}/E(O_N^{\text{€}}) - 1, -X_N^{\text{€}/\$}/E(X_N^{\text{€}/\$}) - 1]$, which is also equal to $-cov[O_N^{\text{€}}/E(O_N^{\text{€}}) - 1, X_N^{\text{€}/\$}/E(X_N^{\text{€}/\$}) - 1]$. The last expression may be restated in terms of two familiar variables: (a) the FX operating exposure to the US dollar, $\gamma_{O\$}^{\text{€}}$; and (b) the volatility of the euro versus the US dollar, $\sigma_{\text{€}}^{\$}$. By definition, $\gamma_{O\$}^{\text{€}} = cov[O_N^{\text{€}}/E(O_N^{\text{€}}) - 1, X_N^{\text{€}/\$}/E(X_N^{\text{€}/\$}) - 1]/[N(\sigma_{\text{€}}^{\$})^2]$. Substituting, we get that $E(O_N^{\$}) = E(O_N^{\text{€}}) \bullet E(X_N^{\$/\text{€}}) + E(O_N^{\text{€}}) \bullet E(X_N^{\$/\text{€}})$ $\left[-N\gamma_{O\$}^{\text{€}}(\sigma_{\text{€}}^{\$})^2\right]$, which simplifies to $E(O_N^{\text{€}}) \bullet E(X_N^{\$/\text{€}})\left[1 - N\gamma_{O\$}^{\text{€}}(\sigma_{\text{€}}^{\$})^2\right]$, which is approximated by equation (4.3).

Chapter 5

1. Some of the material is based on Butler, O'Brien, and Utete (2013).

2. Siegel's paradox is based on the notion $E(X/Y)$ cannot be equal $1/E(Y/X)$, even though $X/Y = 1/(Y/X)$. Equation (5.2) is in Solnik (1993).

3. Estimates of time-0 FX misvaluation are often based on purchasing power parity (PPP) violations, as in the Big Mac Index and adjusted Big Mac Index. See O'Brien (2016), who also shows how to bring in the uncovered interest rate parity (UIRP) condition. This approach could be adjusted to use a version of the UIRP condition with a currency risk premium adjustment like that covered in Chapter 4.

4. Luehrman and Quinn (2010) address this issue in a Harvard case, basing intrinsic FX forecasts on purchasing power parity.

5. See Harris and Ravenscraft (1991); Dewenter (1995); and Erel, Liao, and Weisbach (2012). See also Baker, Foley, and Wurgler (2009), who report that FDI flows increase sharply with source-country stock market valuations.

Chapter 6

1. Start with the linear return-generating model, $R_i^\$ = a_i^\$ + \gamma_{i\euro}^\$ x^{\$/\euro} + \varepsilon_i^\$$, where $\gamma_{i\euro}^\$$ is asset i's FX exposure to the euro. Take the covariance of both sides of this equation with the return on the global market (in US dollars), $R_G^\$$ to get $cov(R_i^\$, R_G^\$) = a_i^\$ + \gamma_{i\euro}^\$ cov(x^{\$/\euro}, R_G^\$) + cov(\varepsilon_i^\$, R_G^\$)$. Divide both sides by the variance of $R_G^\$$, and note that the definition of a beta is covariance with $R_G^\$$, divided by the variance of $R_G^\$$, to get $\beta_i^\$ = \gamma_{i\euro}^\$ \beta_\euro^\$ + \varepsilon_i^\$$. Repeat for asset j to get $\beta_j^\$ = \gamma_{j\euro}^\$ \beta_\euro^\$ + \varepsilon_j^\$$. Subtract the second beta equation from the first and note that if assets i and j have different betas only because of FX exposure, then $\varepsilon_i^\$ = \varepsilon_j^\$$. The result is equation (6.1), where H is \$ and C is \euro.

Bibliography

Abuaf, N. 2011. "Valuing Emerging Market Equities—The Empirical Evidence." *Journal of Applied Finance* 21, no. 2, pp. 123–41.

Abuaf, N. 2015. "Valuing Emerging Market Equities—A Pragmatic Approach Based on the Empirical Evidence." *Journal of Applied Corporate Finance* 25, no. 1, pp. 71–88.

Adler, M., and B. Dumas. 1983. "International Portfolio Choice and Corporate Finance: A Synthesis." *Journal of Finance* 38, no. 3, pp. 925–84.

Adler, M., and P. Jorion. 1992. "Universal Currency Hedges for Global Portfolios." *Journal of Portfolio Management* 18, no. 4, pp. 28–35.

Allayannis, G., J. Ihrig, and J. Weston. 2001. "Exchange-Rate Hedging: Financial vs. Operating Strategies." *American Economic Review Papers & Proceedings* 91, no. 2, pp. 391–95.

Arquette, G., W. Brown, and R. Burdekin. 2008. "Investigating US ADR and Hong Kong H-Share Spreads Against Domestic Shanghai Stock Exchange listings of Chinese firms." *Journal of Banking and Finance* 32, no. 9, pp. 1916–27.

Baker, M., F. Foley, and J. Wurgler. 2009. "Multinationals as Arbitrageurs: The Effect of Stock Market Valuations on Foreign Direct Investment." *Review of Financial Studies* 22, no. 1, pp. 337–89.

Bank of America Roundtable on Evaluating and Financing Foreign Direct Investment. 1996. *Journal of Applied Corporate Finance* 9, no. 3, pp. 64–79.

Baruch, S., A. Karolyi, and M. Lemmon. 2007. "Multimarket Trading and Liquidity: Theory and Evidence." *Journal of Finance* 62, no. 5, pp. 2169–200.

Bates, T., K. Kahle, and R. Stulz. 2009. Why Do U.S. Firms Hold So Much More Cash than They Used To? *Journal of Finance* 64, no. 5, pp. 1985–2022.

Bekaert, G., C. Harvey, C. Lundblad, and S. Siegel. 2016. "Political Risk and International Valuation." *Journal of Corporate Finance* 37, no. 1, pp. 1–23.

Block, S. 2003. "Divisional Cost of Capital: A Study of Its Use by Major U.S. Firms." *Engineering Economist* 48, no. 4, pp. 345–62.

Brotherson, T., K. Eades, R. Harris, and R. Higgins. 2013. "'Best Practices' In Estimating the Cost of Capital: An Update." *Journal of Applied Finance* 23, no. 1, pp. 15–33.

Bruner, R., W. Li, M. Kritzman, S. Myrgren, and S. Page. 2008. "Market Integration in Developed and Emerging Markets: Evidence from the CAPM." *Emerging Markets Review* 9, no. 2, pp. 89–103.

Bryan, A. 2007. "Do ADRs Violate the Law of One Price? Deviations in Price Parity in the Absence of Fundamental Risk." Retrieved February 12, 2013, from Washington University: www.olin.wustl.edu/Documents/CRES/Bryan

Butler, K., T. O'Brien, and G. Utete. 2013. "A Fresh Look at Cross-Border Valuation and FX Hedging Decisions." *Journal of Applied Finance* 23, no. 2, pp. 84–94.

Campbell, J., K. Serfaty-de Medeiros, and L. Viceira. 2010. "Global Currency Hedging." *Journal of Finance* 65, no. 1, pp. 87–121.

Click, R., and R. Weiner. 2010. "Resource Nationalism Meets the Market: Political Risk and the Value of Petroleum Reserves." *Journal of International Business Studies* 41, no. 5, pp. 783–803.

Da, Z., R. Guo, and R. Jagannathan. 2012. "CAPM for Estimating the Cost of Equity Capital: Interpreting the Empirical Evidence." *Journal of Financial Economics* 103, no. 1, pp. 204–20.

Damodaran, A. 2003. "Country Risk and Company Exposure: Theory and Practice." *Journal of Applied Finance* 13, no. 2, pp. 63–75.

de Jong, A., L. Rosenthal, and M. Van Dijk. 2009. "The Risk and Return of Arbitrage in dual-Listed Companies." *Review of Finance* 13, no. 3, pp. 495–520.

Desai, M. 2006. "Globalizing the Cost of Capital and Capital Budgeting at AES." Harvard Business School Case 9–204-109.

Dewenter, K. 1995. "Do Exchange Rate Changes Drive Foreign Direct Investment?" *Journal of Business* 68, no. 3, pp. 406–33.

Donaldson, G., M. Kamstra, and L. Kramer. 2010. "Estimating the Equity Premium." *Journal of Financial and Quantitative Analysis* 45, no. 4, pp. 813–46.

Dumas, B. 1994. "Partial vs. General Equilibrium Models of the International Capital Market." In *The Handbook of International Macroeconomics*, ed. F. van der Ploeg. London: Basil Blackwell.

Erel, I., R. Liao, and M. Weisbach. 2012. "Determinants of Cross-Border Mergers and Acquisitions." *Journal of Finance* 67, no. 3, pp. 1043–81.

Fernandez, P., P. Aguirreamalloa, and L. Avendaño. 2012. US Market Risk Premium Used in 2011 by Professors, Analysts and Companies: A Survey with 5731 Answers. Retrieved February 1, 2013, from SSRN: http://papers.ssrn.com/sol3/papers.cfm?abstract_id=1805852

Froot, K., and E. Dabora. 1999. "How are Stock Prices Affected by the Location of Trade? *Journal of Financial Economics* 53, no. 2, pp. 189–216.

Godfrey, S., and R. Espinosa. 1996. "A Practical Approach to Calculating Costs of Equity for Investments in Emerging Markets." *Journal of Applied Corporate Finance* 9, no. 3, pp. 80–90.

Graham, J. 2000. "How Big are the Tax Benefits of Debt?" *Journal of Finance* 55, no. 5, pp. 1901–41.

Graham, J., and C. Harvey. 2001. "The Theory and Practice of Corporate Finance: Evidence from the Field." *Journal of Financial Economics* 60, no. 2, pp. 187–243.

Halling, M., M. Pagano, O. Randl, and J. Zechner. 2008. "Where Is the Market? Evidence from Cross-Listings in the U.S." *Review of Financial Studies* 21, no. 2, pp. 725–61.

Harris, R., and D. Ravenscraft. 1991. "The Role of Acquisitions in Foreign Direct Investment: Evidence from the U.S. Stock Market." *Journal of Finance* 46, no. 3, pp. 825–44.

Harvey, C. 2000. "The Drivers of Expected Returns in International Markets." *Emerging Markets Quarterly* 4, no. 3, pp. 32–49.

Krapl, A., and T. O'Brien. 2016. "Estimating Cost of Equity: Do You Need to Adjust for Foreign Exchange Risk?" *Journal of International Financial Management & Accounting* 27, no. 1, pp. 5–25.

Krüger, P., A. Landier, and D. Thesmar. 2015. "The WACC Fallacy: The Real Effects of Using a Unique Discount Rate." *Journal of Finance* 70, no. 3, pp. 1253–85.

Lessard, D. 1996. "Incorporating Country Risk in the Valuation of Offshore Projects." *Journal of Applied Corporate Finance* 9, no. 3, pp. 52–63.

Luehrman, T., and P. Heilprin. 2009. "Midland Energy Resources, Inc.: Cost of Capital." Harvard Business School Case 4129.

Luehrman, T., and J. Quinn. 2010. "Groupe Ariel S.A.: Parity Conditions and Crossborder Valuation." Harvard Business School Case 4194.

Lustig, H., and A. Verdelhan. 2011. "The Cross Section of Foreign Currency Risk Premia and Consumption Growth Risk: Reply." *American Economic Review* 101, no. 7, pp. 3477–3500.

Maldonado, R., and A. Saunders. 1983. "Foreign Exchange Restrictions and the Law of One Price." *Financial Management* 12, no. 1, pp. 19–23.

Mei, J., J. Scheinkman, and W. Xiong. 2009. "Speculative Trading and Stock Price: Evidence from Chinese A-B Share Premia." *Annals of Economics and Finance* 10, no. 2, pp. 225–55.

Miles, J., and R. Ezzell. 1980. "The Weighted Average Cost of Capital, Perfect Capital Markets, and Project Life: A Clarification." *Journal of Financial and Quantitative Analysis* 15, no. 3, pp. 719–30.

Miller, M. 1977. "Debt and Taxes." *Journal of Finance* 32, no. 2, pp. 261–75.

Miller, M., and F. Modigliani. 1963. "Corporate Income Taxes and the Cost of Capital: A Correction." *American Economic Review* 53, no. 3, pp. 433–43.

O'Brien, T. 2016. *Introduction to Foreign Exchange Rates.* 2nd ed. New York, NY: Business Expert Press.

O'Brien, T. 2017. *Applied International Finance I: Managing Foreign Exchange Risk.* 2nd ed. New York, NY: Business Expert Press.

Perold, A. 2004. "The Capital Asset Pricing Model." *Journal of Economic Perspectives* 18, no. 3, pp. 3–24.

Pettit, J., M. Ferguson, and R. Gluck. 1999. "A Method for Estimating Corporate Capital Costs: The Case of Bestfoods." *Journal of Applied Corporate Finance* 12, no. 3, pp. 80–90.

Ross, S., and M. Walsh. 1983. "A Simple Approach to the Pricing of Risky Assets with Uncertain Exchange Rates." In *Research in International Business and Finance,* eds. R. Hawkins, R. Levich, and C. Wihlborg et al., 39–54. Vol 3. Greenwich, CT: JAI Press.

Sercu, P. 1980. "A Generalization of the International Asset Pricing Model." *Revue de l'Association Francaise de Finance* 1, no. 1, pp. 91–135.

Solnik, B. 1974. "An Equilibrium Model of the International Capital Market." *Journal of Economic Theory* 8, no. 4, pp. 500–24.

Solnik, B. 1993. "Currency Hedging and Siegel's Paradox: On Black's Universal Hedging Rule." *Review of International Economics* 1, no. 2, pp. 180–87.

Solnik, B. 1997. "The World Price of Foreign Exchange Risk: Some Synthetic Comments." *European Financial Management* 3, no. 1, pp. 9–22.

Stulz, R. 1995a. "Globalization of Capital Markets and the Cost of Capital: The Case of Nestlé." *Journal of Applied Corporate Finance* 8, no. 3, pp. 30–38.

Stulz, R. 1995b. "The Cost of Capital in Internationally Integrated Markets: The Case of Nestlé." *European Financial Management* 1, no. 1, pp. 11–22.

Welch, I. 2009. "The Consensus Estimate for the Equity Premium by Academic Financial Economists in December 2007.Retrieved June 1, 2013, from SSRN: http://papers.ssrn.com/sol3/papers.cfm?abstract_id=1084918

Weston, F. 1973. "Investment Decisions Using the Capital Asset Pricing Model." *Financial Management* 2, no. 1, pp. 25–33.

Zenner, M., and E. Akaydin. 2002. *A Practical Approach to the International Valuation and Capital Allocation Puzzle.* New York, NY: Salomon Smith Barney.

Index

OTHER TITLES IN OUR FINANCE AND FINANCIAL MANAGEMENT COLLECTION

John A. Doukas, Old Dominion University, Editor

Announcing the Business Expert Press Digital Library

Concise e-books business students need for classroom and research

CPSIA information can be obtained
at www.ICGtesting.com
Printed in the USA
FFOW01n2310090718
47321086-50329FF

9 781631 579226